Intentional Ministry

Intentional Ministry

Tim Gehle, C.Ed.D

Corridor 314, LLC

2018

First Printing: 2018

ISBN 978-0-692-14301-8

Corridor 314, LLC

9955 E. Greenway St.

Mesa, AZ 85207

www.corridor314.com

Dedication

To Rhonda: Without your encouragement, I would not have had the courage to explore and ultimately accept the position where I learned this process. It is amazing to see the doors God has opened because you encouraged me to step out of my comfort zone and try. Thank you for your patience, confidence, skills, and support. This work would not have come to pass without you. I love you fiercely!

Acknowledgements

To David: The graphics make the model come to life. Thanks for the gift of your time and talents to make that happen. I am in your debt.

To the Piloting Church: Thank you for taking the risk to allow me to translate this educational model into the ministry world. I am humbled by the faith you placed in me. Blessings to you!

Contents

Contents

Part 1: Theory and Fundamentals

A basic understanding of the theory and rationale that support a model helps the user of the model act with confidence by knowing that the model has been thoughtfully considered. It is also significantly important to understand the structure of the model before attempting to implement it. The three chapters that follow are dedicated to providing the theoretical support, rationale, and requisite overview of the Intentional Ministry Model.

Chapter 1:

Theoretical Foundations

Outcomes Based Education

When it was first conceived, the notion of outcomes based education was not well received by educators and parents across the United States as many feared that individual student differences would be discounted or ignored as all students would be required to learn the same things to the same degree of proficiency. Outcomes based education also was problematic in assessing the affective domain of learning.

With the work of Wiggins and McTighe (1998) came a significant shift in the conceptualization and development of K-12 curriculum and the attitude toward outcomes based education. Their work is considered by most educators as a foundational work in modern curriculum design. Rooted in the most positive aspects of outcomes based education, the concept is simple: determine what you want students to know and be able to do when they complete the unit, course, grade, or program, and work backwards to what they need to know and do today in order to reach that ultimate goal. This model of backwards design is a simple notion that reframes outcomes based education and displays profound implications for not only educators, but also for developers of ministries. The Intentional Ministry Model, then, extends the work of Wiggins and McTighe by applying the concept of outcomes based education to program or ministry development, a new and otherwise unintended arena of application. Nonetheless, outcomes based education remains a secular model that does not account for the spiritual dimension encountered in the design of ministry. This lack of spirituality necessitates adaptations to the general model of outcomes based education which, as will be seen in the pages that follow, become the basis of the Intentional Ministry Model.

Intentional Ministry

Ministry development is ever as complex as curriculum development and also carries with it some unique challenges including integrating concepts of affective and emotional development, spiritual inputs, and a perpetual learning environment rather than a finite environment such as a course or degree program. The Intentional Ministry Model is designed to account for these challenges by both building on the notion of outcomes based education and applying its foundational concepts to an entirely different discipline for which outcomes based education was not designed. The Intentional Ministry Model is grounded in the spiritual disciplines of prayer and the seeking of wisdom. It is focused on people made in God's image and reflects in finite space His infinite nature by acknowledging that ministry should not end; though people move in and out of ministries on a regular basis, the ministry continues.

The Intentional Ministry Model also considers Gaebelein's (1985) assertion that God is the source of all truth. Thus, the truth stemming from logic and reason, aptitudes applied in intentional ministry design, can be seen to emanate from God and not to be shunned. God has given man the ability to reason. While one must be cautious to avoid complete reliance on the intellect, logic, and reason of fallen man to the neglect of Godly, spiritual input, logic and reason are also gifts from God and need not be feared. Ultimately, in a choice to follow man's logic or the leading of the Spirit of God, the wisdom of God and the leading of His Spirit trump the intellect and logic of man at every turn. The Intentional Ministry Model affirms this concept. Being founded on prayer and the earnest seeking of God's will for an organization and promoting ongoing, constant, prayerful evaluation throughout the design process and into program or ministry implementation, the Intentional Ministry Model provides a means to allow God-given reason and divine leading to flourish together simultaneously and harmoniously.

Contrast of Outcomes Based Education and Intentional Ministry

When comparing outcomes based education to intentional ministry, there are several key points of contrast. These areas of contrast have to do with the disciplines in which each model is applied and the nature of those disciplines. The contrasts extend to the duration of the design use and the primary means of evaluation in each discipline. Specifically, outcomes based education is generally considered a concept applied to K-12 education while the Intentional Ministry Model is applied to the design of Christian ministries.

Finite v. Infinite Systems

The K-12 model is a finite system. Ideally, students begin at Kindergarten and progress through the required years of study culminating at the end of grade 12 at which time they graduate from the program having symbolically and, hopefully realistically, attained to the level of proficiency anticipated in the design of the educational program. In this model, the majority of students complete their studies in roughly the same time span and at approximately the same chronologic age. Some may begin earlier and/or end later, but the system remains finite with a set number of distinct levels through which all students must pass. There is not another level in this system; the system ends at grade 12 making it a finite system. If outcomes based education has functioned as intended, all students graduate at essentially the same point in their lifespans having internalized relatively the same body of knowledge.

Some universities are now applying outcomes based educational design to their programs. However, these systems remain finite systems with distinct beginning and completion points. Consider undergraduate education, for example. Students in a given program/major take largely the same set of courses with only minor differences in the form of elective courses or, perhaps, variation from alternate tracks such as honors programs that address the same information but impose on the student additional requirements. In all cases, however, students complete these programs in a similar, finite amount of time based on the number of required credit hours. Some may take more or less chronological time depending on personal circumstances, but the system remains finite with a set number of credits that must be earned to reach completion. Even with modern delivery systems such as online education, the system remains finite based on the required number of credits to complete the program.

Contrast this system with most ministry systems, and the relatively infinite nature of ministry is quickly seen. Granted, there are traditional teaching ministries aligned with the K-12 grades, but unlike a K-12 school system, the ministry system continues beyond the grade 12 equivalent and through the entirety of adulthood. Thus, ministry is a much more infinite system since it has no fixed ending point. By means of example, consider ministries such as the

Adult Teaching Ministry that extends for multiple decades; music ministry where individuals may enter prior to attending kindergarten and continue to serve, learn, and grow for the rest of their lives; or even a ministry to Baby Boomers that will follow this generation throughout their lives. In these examples, some participants in the ministry become the next generation of leaders raising up another generation of leaders who in turn raise up yet another generation of leaders and so on infinitely until Christ's return and His ultimate perfecting of the believers.

The implications of the infinite nature of ministry directly influence the design of ministry. Ministry designers cannot expect that all individuals will attain to one fixed set of competencies at relatively the same time and level of expertise. Confound this further with the notion that not all individuals in a ministry are called to or desirous of advancement beyond a certain level of competency, and the relatively infinite nature is an obvious factor in the design of ministry. The result is that ministry requires an adaptation of the outcomes based education model in order to meet the needs of those the ministry serves and who will ultimately perpetuate the ministry by entering service themselves.

The primary adaptation is in the structure of the outcomes. While finite outcomes work well in a finite system such as the K-12 environment, a relatively infinite system such as ministry requires the development of infinitely structured outcomes. These outcomes must remain measurable in order for leaders to determine the success or failure of a ministry, but they must also remain challenging enough, even somewhat unattainable, to keep the participants engaged over the relatively infinite span of the ministry. Addressing the relatively infinite nature of ministry is one role of the Intentional Ministry Model.

Quantitative v. Qualitative Frameworks

Evaluation of outcomes based education as seen in the K-12 or university models is based dominantly in quantitative research methods. This is not to imply that there are no qualitative methods employed in the evaluation of outcomes based education. However, the system was designed to allow for quantitative research methodology to be applied as such methodology was deemed to be more objective and, thus, more appropriate for this type of system. Using the K-12 system as a model, this logic is reasonable as K-12 educators and educational leaders continue to strive to bolster the reputation of the discipline of education and to bring it into alignment with the respected scientific research methods of other disciplines. This requires rooting the design of the system in quantitative, empirical methodology.

To this end, outcomes based education uses measurements that are objective and quantifiable. These measurements include high school proficiency exams, college entrance exams, state achievement tests, classroom evaluations, and even assignment and course grades. All of these instruments may include affective questions in segments that are subjectively graded. However, even seemingly subjective components of these evaluations are commonly governed by grading rubrics in an attempt to make them more objective and to unify scoring. Ultimately, all of these measurements lead to Likert-style scales expressing the level of proficiency of each student so that quantitative statistical analyses can be applied to determine the success or failure of each individual, group, or program. These analyses may be accurate and relatively objective, and they may serve the needs of the given program. However, though there is a shared goal of improving individuals and programs, Christian ministry simply functions differently than K-12 or university education.

While outcomes based education is finite and its assessment rooted in quantitative research, ministry is infinite and tends to employ qualitative research methods. While ministry evaluation may use elements of quantitative research to measure its outcomes, the dominant forms of ministry evaluation remain qualitative. These methods include observation of behavior, participation in ministry, and personal growth as well as the rise of individuals to the role of teacher/trainer. As noted, some elements of quantitative research may be employed in the evaluation of ministry. For example, simple measurement of numbers of people participating in a given ministry is a meaningful quantitative measure. However, this measurement does not mean that the ministry is successful. The success of a ministry is more closely related to the depth of an individual's spiritual encounter, the identifiable personal growth in character and application of life principles, the building and strengthening of interpersonal relationships, and the development of leaders to train the next generation and sustain the ministry. Thus, the spiritual, emotional, and social nature of ministry and the necessary focus toward the affective domain of learning and outcomes requires a different approach that is largely qualitative in nature. The Intentional Ministry Model accounts for the spiritual aspect and the qualitative nature of the evaluation.

The qualitative nature of the evaluation of ministry also implies a necessary adaptation to the design of the outcomes so that qualitative measures can be applied in meaningful ways. While the outcomes must remain measurable, measurement will commonly be accomplished by observation, interview, and other qualitative methods. All of these methods require the evaluator to remain focused on the displayed behaviors of the ministry participants. The evaluator must ask questions related to the perceived happiness of participants; their sense of accomplishment, value, and self-worth; and their perceived and demonstrated spiritual growth. The evaluator may also seek to determine to what extent ministry participants display characteristics and dispositions that are aligned to biblical truth and the doctrines of the ministry. The

Intentional Ministry Model allows for these forms of measurement.

Ministry Is Spiritual

Perhaps the greatest difference between outcomes based education and ministry is the spiritual nature of ministry. While both outcomes based education and the Intentional Ministry Model naturally reflect the philosophy of the designers using the models, ministry cannot be effectively developed without distinctly spiritual considerations including significant time in prayer, searching the Word of God, and seeking God's will for the prospective ministry. If the ministry is not in alignment with the will of God for a given church or parachurch organization, it is destined to fail regardless of the level of planning that is involved. The Intentional Ministry Model accounts for this spiritual underpinning by placing prayer and searching the Word of God as central and foundational to the remaining considerations of ministry design. Project participants and other stakeholders employ prayer, searching the Word of God, and seeking God's will through the duration of the ministry design lest the ministry designers succumb to personal tastes and whims rather than serving as vessels of God's plan in the design of the ministry.

The fundamental spiritual requirements of ministry design necessitate special considerations for the appointment of members to the ministry design group. Note that this group is not referred to as a design "team." Since the Church is identified as the "body of Christ," (1 Cor. 12:27) the design group ought to be considered a system of the body and function in the close relationship that implies rather than merely purporting to be a team with all of its secular implications. When one considers that Acts 6:3 indicates that even a task so seemingly menial as waiting tables required individuals to demonstrate evidence of being "full of the Spirit and wisdom," how much more significant is the design of ministry than the waiting of tables. How much more care ought to be taken, then, in the selection of the designers? That is not to say that the individuals involved should represent a homogenous group of vocational pastors. Quite to the contrary, the design group ought to be as diverse as the church or organization and the ministry the group will create. It is recommended that the design group include pastoral leadership, lay leadership, interested parties, and potential participants. The group should also contain at least one individual skilled in applying the Intentional Ministry Model who can act as a facilitator to keep the design process moving forward. The facilitator may or may not have expertise in the particular ministry to be designed, but contributes the working knowledge of applying the Intentional Ministry Model both by knowing what questions are appropriate to ask at each point in the process and by knowing when to allow the group to think, vent, or process as well as when to encourage forward movement to avoid becoming mired. The last portion of this book will address the application of the Intentional Ministry Model in order to provide at least minimal exposure to the model's implementation.

Chapter 2:

Why Intentional Ministry?

Introduction

At this point, it is reasonable to wonder why the Intentional Ministry Model is necessary. After all, there are a plethora of ready-made and pre-packaged ministries and programs that churches and parachurch organizations can simply use on a "plug-and-play" basis without the extra effort of engaging in ministry design. These include ministries and programs for children, youth, and even Baby Boomers. In some instances, the institution of a new ministry or program is considered accomplished through something as simple as delegating an individual to launch the new ministry. So the question of why one should bother to engage in ministry design remains a viable concern.

Current State of Ministry Preparation and Planning

The origin of new ministries or programs is commonly associated with the strategic planning process. During this process, churches and parachurch organizations commonly engage in much soul searching and prayer as leaders seek to identify needs that the ministry or organization can and should fill as part of their mission to the local community and the Church universal. These identified needs are typically targeted toward reaching a given population segment or to fulfilling a particular function in the church or organization. In some instances, leaders know the need is there, write it into the strategic plan, and intend to do something though they do not know precisely how to accomplish the goal. The result is that leaders may either table any action on the need or delve into extended discussions of possible methods for meeting the strategic plan only to eventually conclude that some action, even if imperfect or ill-conceived, must be taken to meet the strategic plan goal. The church or organization then launches into a new program or ministry somewhat blindly hoping for good results while remaining uncertain how to determine if the results are indeed good. In this situation, doing something is viewed as better than inaction even if the results of the initiative are ultimately deemed unfavorable.

Thus, the institution of a new ministry or program, while potentially following this lengthy period of strategic planning to determine that the ministry is necessary, is often considered accomplished at the point of delegating an individual to launch and lead the ministry or program. Considerations of design, structure, and evaluation are not present as leaders assume that the delegated individual will see to whatever is needed to make the ministry or program function. From here, church and organization leaders often step away feeling confident in their actions, being convinced that the ministry or program will be a success because of the individual in control, and leaving the delegated individual to affirm these feelings and beliefs. This individual may conceptualize ministry as a series of events and proceed wholeheartedly into planning out the first of those events – typically a large "kick-off" event designed to draw a crowd, acquaint them with the purpose of the ministry, and pique their interest in returning for the next event. From here, ministry is believed to happen within each unique event, and the ministry or program leader is supported but left alone so long as the planned events are well attended.

At times, little or no ministry design is involved. These instances tend to occur when leaders feel obligated to react somewhat hastily to certain types of situations. In one scenario, leadership may be approached by one or more individuals who expound on a felt need and wonder how the leadership will move to meet that need often on threat of dissociation with the church or parachurch organization if nothing is done. In this instance, the individual with the grand idea may be seeking an opportunity to enter the leadership ranks or may simply be attempting to exercise some level of authority which he or she has not been accorded. Too often, leaders buckle to the veiled threat and launch into a ministry or program that may not fit the goals and direction of the organization simply to prevent the loss of an individual or small group of individuals. In another scenario, the felt need is couched in more spiritual terms by an individual member or leader who believes he or she has had a personal, spiritual revelation of the need and uses the "God told me we need to <insert ministry or program idea here>" argument in hopes of compelling leadership to launch a new ministry or program. Often, leadership will launch the ministry or program without additional planning lest they be viewed as unspiritual or disobedient to God. The concern with both of these situations is not necessarily in the suggestion itself. In the first scenario, it is in the means of delivering the suggestion and the implied threat undergirding it. In the second case, it is in the opportunistic motivation of the one making the suggestion. Of course, in the best case scenario, veiled threats and opportunistic intentions are completely lacking; God may well have laid a ministry or program on the heart of an individual who was bold enough to share it in hope of opening a door for the Spirit of God to work in the lives of people the church or organization is desiring to reach. In all cases, the issue is not the idea but the response to the idea. In these instances, organization leaders are prone to respond without considering how the proposed program fits into the strategic plan for the church or organization let alone how the ministry or program will be designed. This somewhat "off-the-cuff" approach will lead to missed opportunities at best and utter failure of the ministry or program at worst.

Current Evaluation Techniques

In many, though certainly not all, church and parachurch organizations, formal evaluation of ministries or programs is minimal to non-existent. Many leaders simply do not consider it necessary to formally evaluate ministries or programs. The unstated reason is often that the organization was directed by God to enter into the ministry or program, so it will continue to operate the ministry or program until such time as God directs otherwise. Evaluation is simply not necessary. Other leaders avoid evaluation using the same unstated reasoning above, but the reasoning is founded in an underlying notion that they are unworthy to evaluate a ministry or program that God instituted in their midst and of which they are merely stewards. Evaluation is simply not proper. Painfully, it must also be admitted that some leaders are not cognizant of the notion of evaluating ministries or programs and, therefore, do not even engage in the unstated reasoning described above. Evaluation is simply not in the vocabulary.

Nonetheless, nearly every organization seeks to determine by some means whether the program or ministry is actually working. Most Christian organizations genuinely want to know they are being successful and pleasing God. This dichotomy is, then, most often addressed by superficial measures backed by anecdotal information. For example, with no means to measure the effectiveness of the program or ministry, the easiest method to gauge its purported success is to examine the volume of attendees at events sponsored by the program or ministry; in this model, more people in attendance means greater success. In reality, there are much stronger measures that could and should be employed to determine effectiveness, but without stated goals, invoking stronger measurements based in objective data is not possible. So, organizational leaders do the next best thing and invoke pseudo-qualitative measures in the form of anecdotal information. This is commonly expressed by the program or ministry leader exclaiming how one individual is testifying of a life changed or that the leader has noticed what seems to be many of the same attendees over a given period. Coupled with an increase in attendance numbers, the program or ministry must be doing well, right? While even a single changed life makes operating a program of ministry worth doing, how much more effective, how many more lives could be changed, if we approached ministries and programs with a focused intention and could harness solid data to support what was intuitively felt or anecdotally expressed?

In any case and for whatever reason, even the most well-meaning organizations fall short when they fail to be intentional in the design of the ministry or program by not determining desired outcomes during the planning stage. Simply stated, where there is no intention, there is legitimately no means by which to measure the success or failure of the ministry or program. This is the unfortunate state of some, if not many, ministries or programs operated by churches and parachurch organizations.

Living in a World without Intention

Launching into a ministry or program without intentionally designing the program potentially leads to significant negative consequences. One of the significant consequences is the lack of available formative and summative data to guide the ministry into the success that God intends for it. For those who may be unfamiliar with the concepts, further explanation of formative and summative data is presented in the following paragraph. Another critical result of ignoring intentional design principles is the "moving target syndrome" in which change happens seemingly for the sole sake of change with no real focus.

Formative data is information used throughout the operation of a program or ministry to determine if it is moving the right direction. Formative data allows for the illumination of positive and negative aspects of the program or ministry so that small corrections can be made to keep the ministry or program moving toward its intended goals. Formative data is gathered in an ongoing manner and may be gathered informally as it remains grounded in the intentions of the ministry or program rather than simply being anecdotal. Summative data is gathered more formally and on larger intervals than formative data. For example, a yearly evaluation of the program will yield summative data. Summative data is used to determine whether the ministry or program is meeting the intended goals and outcomes, and this data may determine whether the organization should continue to operate the program or ministry.

Without formative and summative data, organizational leaders have no means of making appropriate real time corrections to a program or ministry. Indeed, they have no means to determine if the ministry or program is working at all. The result is, at best, the continued use of anecdotal assessment such as testimonials of a small handful of individuals who are wholeheartedly impressed by the program or ministry as well as those who have legitimately had their lives changed by the program or ministry. Other perfunctory means such as tracking attendance and sensing that the same individuals may regularly be attending events sponsored by the program or ministry may also be invoked as no other meaningful data can be gathered since the intention of the ministry or program is not known. At worst, absolutely no assessment of ministries or programs is conducted.

Another unwitting result of launching into a ministry or program without intentional planning is that changes to the ministry or program tend to be frequent and can feel somewhat random. Where there is no concept of the intended outcomes, changes may or may not lead to improvement. More often than not, these random changes lead to missed opportunities for real improvement and continued growth. These missed opportunities may manifest themselves as poorly timed decisions. In this case, decisions to change may occur too quickly or too slowly. For example, where there is no outcome to measure whether the program is actually effective, leaders commonly revert to the attendance component to determine if the program or ministry is successful. If attendance does not seem to be growing as quickly as expected despite a program or ministry having only operated for a brief time, leaders may become impatient and determine to change the meeting time and day in hopes of drawing additional participants. The reality may be that the program or ministry is highly effective, but without intentional outcomes established, this cannot be seen. The change occurs too quickly, and the opportunity for solid, meaningful growth is missed. Conversely, a program or ministry may appear to be growing at a rate better than expected, so leaders allow the program to continue to function without change for an extended period of time. Were there established outcomes, the data would indicate that the program is highly ineffective and the attendance is merely an indication of an alternative outcome such as perceived social connection that, while good in and of itself, is not what the program or ministry was put in place to accomplish. In reality, change is necessary for the program to be effective, but it is happening too slowly. The opportunity for making effective change to create a healthy program or ministry is missed. In a worse case, the missed opportunity manifests itself as a fully wrong decision. For example, leaders are approached with an option to expand the ministry or program into another area that is related but outside the scope of the program or ministry. Without intended outcomes to guide them, leaders wrongly choose to expand the ministry or program into an area that is not part of its core mission. Because the program or ministry was never intended to enter this area but there are no identified outcomes to guide the thought process, the decision is enacted and effectively dooms the program or ministry to failure missing the opportunity for genuine success because the program or ministry fails.

Living in a World of Intention

Imagine a world where programs and ministries are highly effective and the work of the program or ministry is efficient and orderly, maximizing the strengths of leaders and laypersons as well as policy makers and policy implementers. Imagine leading a program or ministry that runs well without feeling overly programmed because it is grounded in a clear connection to the mission, vision, and core values of the organization. This is a different world. This is the world of intentional ministry.

The Intentional Ministry Model creates planned programs and ministries that deliberately meet felt needs. This planning gives leaders a sense of security and allows them to confidently delegate routine operations to implementation crews who can carry out the work with resolve. Planned programs allow leaders to set reasonable expectations for operations and eliminate the guess work and the constant, random adjustments to programs or ministries thus reducing leader stress. Planned programs allow for shared vision and mission among leaders and implementers thus enhancing a sense of community and allowing a shared leadership model to flourish.

The Intentional Ministry Model offers a structure to programs or ministries. Structure gives boundaries for leaders and implementers allowing both to work freely and flexibly within established guidelines. This type of structure eliminates the need for micromanagement, freeing program or ministry leaders to concentrate on higher-level leadership activities while being comfortable that the program or ministry can function appropriately under the guidance of implementers who are charged with the work. This reduces stress on program or ministry leaders by building shared leadership between leaders and implementers maximizing the gifts, talents, and abilities of both groups.

The Intentional Ministry Model, by the nature of its design process, assures that each program or ministry is aligned with and promotes the mission, vision, and core values of the organization. It deliberately examines each program or ministry opportunity in light of the mission, vision, and values of the organization and overtly asks whether the program or ministry aligns to these characteristics. Those programs or ministries that align well are further developed while those that do not align well are re-worked to align directly, discarded, or offered to other organizations where the concepts may more closely align to the mission, vision, and core values. The alignment to an organization's mission, vision, and values allows leaders and implementers to engage enthusiastically with the program or ministry given the assurance that the work they are doing is meaningful to the organization and the core audience it serves.

In addition, the Intentional Ministry Model provides measurable outcomes. Measurable outcomes are the basis for objective assessment of programs and ministries. They provide a solid, rational, and logical means of measurement in contrast to reliance on anecdotal information or "gut feelings" that a ministry or program is or is not flourishing. By establishing intended outcomes prior to implementing the program or ministry, leadership has evidence by which to determine the success or failure of a program or ministry. The practice of simply observing numbers of attendees or hearing that people are happy is replaced with data that leaders can use to make informed decisions. The data gathered by measuring specific intended outcomes is formative as well as summative in nature. That is, leaders can use the data to make adaptive decisions (formative) as well as overall evaluations (summative) of the program or ministry. The use of formative assessments allows for the timely implementation of change. The change may be preventive, steering the program or ministry away from a potentially harmful situation. It may be adaptive, taking a program or ministry that is working relatively well and adapting it for greater efficiency. It may also be innovative, taking a program or ministry that is functioning at a high level of efficiency and success and adjusting it to align with a new or trending nuance in the community served or in societal behaviors. The existence of measurable outcomes also allows for summative evaluation whereby leaders can make larger decisions regarding whether a program or ministry is truly successful in its intensions and should be continued or whether the program or ministry is simply not working and should be abandoned.

Why Not Be Intentional?

A simple lack of experience with intentional planning deters most organizations from engaging in the intentional design of programs and ministries. Many pastors, lay leaders, and organizational leaders have not heard of such an option and consequently do not have the practical training and expertise to design programs. However, this ought not to be a deterrent as intentional design can be learned. Just as strategic planning for the business and ministry goals and targets is a learned skill, so also is ministry and program design a learned skill. While intentional design of ministry and programs does require a level of expertise, the skill can be learned by pastors, lay leaders, and organizational leaders who are interested in enhancing the ministries and programs offered and helping to assure the focused delivery and meaningful assessment of these ministries and programs.

Once aware that the option exists, perhaps the most common reason for not engaging in intentional design is that it takes time. For many organizations, the need is considered urgent and the desire to act quickly drives their actions. The reality is that intentional design takes time but is not vastly different from the overall amount of time required to implement pre-packaged programs. These types of ready-made programs often involve extensive staff training that can delay implementation. In addition, some organizations find it necessary to change programs as readily as every year or two because the pre-packaged programs do not always transfer to varied populations. Conversely, ministries or programs created through intentional design will tend to have a longer duration of usefulness including a review cycle that allows for adjustments to be made. This reduces time and resource needs in the long term as intentional design allocates the initial time requirements differently. Instead of using the common model of an instructional conference where leaders are trained and return to train others to do the work of the program, intentional design uses a collaborative approach that engages a cross-section of stakeholders and creates long range support for the program or ministry. The hours spent learning someone else's ideas in a conference followed by implementation activities are simply allocated differently but with the results being a custom program or ministry designed to function in the environment of the organization.

Nonetheless, for some organizations, the financial constraints of learning to do intentional ministry and program design remain daunting. Not for profit organizations and ministries often function on highly limited budgets, so securing training in intentional design or hiring expert consultants seems an impossibility. Experts cost money. The intentional design of ministries or programs costs money. However, when the cost of training in intentional design or hiring an expert in intentional design are considered in relation to the costs of re-instituting new programs at often brief intervals, the cost of intentional design can be significantly less. The difference is in the longevity of an intentionally designed program or ministry. Instead of spending large amounts of money every few months or couple of years to train staff to implement a new program that may or may not meet the needs and goals of the ministry or organization, leaders are wise to invest in a singular instance of the intentional design of programs and ministries. The intentional design of a program or ministry will not need to be comprehensively repeated as will the implementation of pre-packaged program models that may fail because they were not specifically intended to address the interpersonal nuances of the settings in which they are applied. Simply stated, programs or ministries intentionally developed specifically for the ministry or organization will tend to have longer lifespans and save money in the longer term. This requires a paradigm shift in many organizations that focus on the immediate cash flow to the exclusion, often out of necessity, of longer range planning and preparation. However, it is a shift well worth making as the long range benefits far outweigh the costs and can be more cost effective leaving additional resources for the work of the organization.

For some organizations, investing into an intentional ministry design can be fearful as the design includes a plan for evaluation of the ministry or program and raises questions related to what happens if the evaluation of the ministry or program is not favorable. Reconciling unfavorable information about a program or ministry gathered during an evaluation cycle with extending grace, showing compassion, and reflecting a Christ-like attitude can seem daunting. However, by developing into the design of the program or ministry clearly established intended outcomes and both formative and summative assessment measures, the model allows leaders to engage in ongoing adjustments and long-range evaluation, respectively. Intentional design also creates an objective stance that allows organizations to review programs or ministries as unique entities in and of themselves rather than as emotional appendages of individuals even when the evaluation reveals that a program or ministry is ineffective, misaligned to the organization, or simply not necessary for one reason or another. Indeed, intentional design actually reduces the likelihood of the program or ministry falling into one of those categories because of the objective formative assessments that allow for quick midstream adjustments to the program or ministry in lieu of completely abandoning the program or ministry.

Nonetheless, the move to intentional design remains somewhat daunting because it involves a significant paradigm shift that includes being willing to embark on a new adventure of faith to trust God in different ways and for different things than in the past. The good news is that the obstacles discussed can be overcome allowing leaders to pursue intentionality wholeheartedly.

Strategic Planning and Intentional Ministry

The presence of a strategic plan for the organization is vastly different from the intentional design of a program or ministry within the organization. Nonetheless, some organizational leaders or stakeholders may use the presence of a strategic plan to assert that intentional design is not necessary. In reality, both strategic planning and intentional design are critical to organizational success and should not be considered as synonymous.

The primary distinction between strategic planning and intentional design is the timing for implementing the tactic. Strategic planning is broad, overall planning for an organization. It provides a framework for the organization to determine why it exists (mission) and how it will accomplish its purposes (vision). Strategic planning establishes goals for the organization and reasonable timelines for addressing and attaining those goals. Strategic planning is the vehicle for determining when and if a program or ministry is necessary within the organization. For example, a strategic plan indicates that over the next year the organization will implement a program for training new parents in child care or a ministry to Baby Boomers. The strategic plan comes first making the need for the program or ministry known and establishing a timeline for bringing it to pass. Once the determination to implement a program or ministry is made, the program or ministry must be designed. This is where the Intentional Ministry Model applies; it is a design model that allows an organization to effectively develop a program or ministry and the means to evaluate it. So, the design of the program or ministry follows from the strategic plan decision to create the program or ministry. The Intentional Ministry Model begins with the perceived need and desire to create and implement a program or ministry that will help the organization reach its goals outlined in the strategic plan. From there, the model addresses the intended outcomes of the program or ministry, how to structure the program or ministry to meet those outcomes, and how to objectively engage in both formative and summative evaluation for the continuous improvement, health, and longevity of the program or ministry.

It should be clear that organizations should engage in both strategic planning and intentional design. The two concepts are not synonymous; they are complementary. While strategic planning determines what program or ministry to offer, when to offer it, and how to fund it, application of intentional design through the Intentional Ministry Model articulates how the program or ministry connects to the mission, vision, and core values of the organization as established in the strategic plan; articulates measurable outcomes so the program or ministry has a clear focus; and creates both objective evaluation criteria and an objective evaluation plan for the program or ministry.

Chapter 3:

The Intentional Ministry Model Explained

Assembling the Participants

The Intentional Ministry Model is a collaborative model; it requires multiple inputs from multiple sources to assure maximum effectiveness. Therefore, before enacting the Model, leaders should assemble a group of core individuals who will serve throughout the process. These individuals should represent the varied stakeholder groups within the church or organization. The commitment required may be for a few months or, in some extreme cases, up to a year or more. In any case, participants should be chosen who have a vested interest in the ministry or program, who oversee or participate in complementary ministries or programs, or who simply have a passion for ministry and a heart to engage in the process.

In addition, it is wise to have at least one project participant who is familiar with the Intentional Ministry Model or who has experience in ministry, program, or even curriculum design. This individual should serve as the project manager or project facilitator whether that service is paid or voluntary. In situations where an experienced program design individual is not readily available among the stakeholders, it makes sense to secure the services of an external consultant who has familiarity with program or ministry design and who will serve as the project manager/facilitator.

Project participants fill two general roles: process oversight and content creation. Process oversight rests with the project manager/facilitator who is charged with assuring that the process runs smoothly and continues to move forward. The project manager/facilitator should report directly to the senior leader of the organization or the leader's delegate to the project. This allows the manager/facilitator to oversee process without undue challenge from other participants. While the project manager/facilitator need not have expertise in the specific ministry or program being created, he or she must understand the process well enough to ask the appropriate questions in a timely manner including questioning content that seems contextually inappropriate or misplaced. In addition, the manager/facilitator should be a good listener and possess the ability to synthesize ideas from multiple inputs in real time to keep the process moving ahead. The remaining participants are collectively responsible for the creation of program content. These individuals must be able to reason well and to bring creative ideas to the group for consideration and critical review. They must be able to remain emotionally neutral as needed in order to critically appraise their own ideas and the ideas of others without becoming offended, yet they must remain passionate about the development of the program and willing to defend ideas that are challenged when such defense is merited.

Overview of the Model

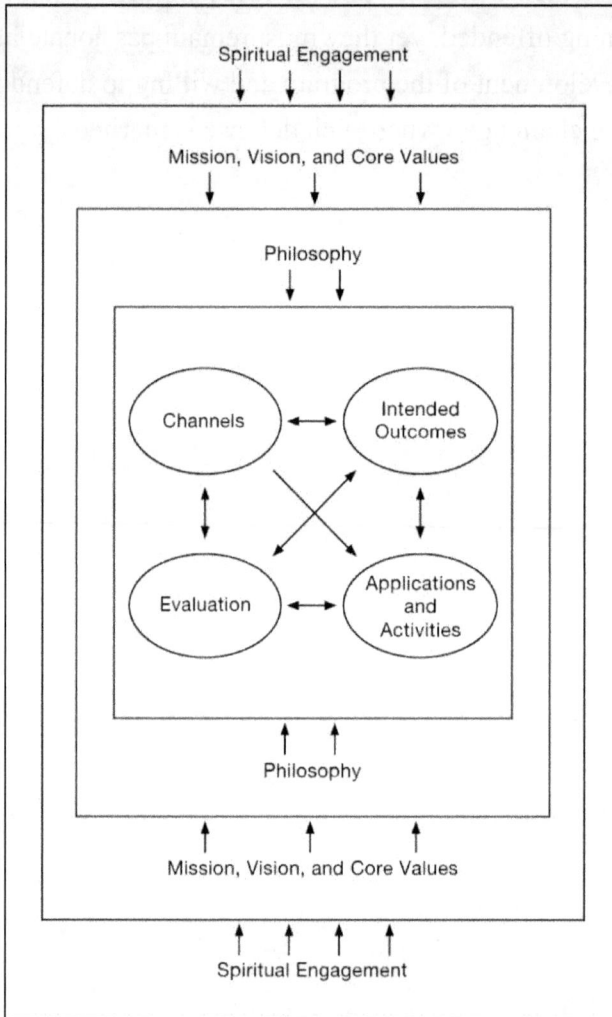

Spiritual Engagement

Mission, Vision, and Core Values

Philosophy

Channels ↔ Intended Outcomes

Evaluation ↔ Applications and Activities

Philosophy

Mission, Vision, and Core Values

Spiritual Engagement

The Intentional Ministry Model is comprised of seven steps. The steps are as follows:

1. Spiritual Engagement
2. Mission, Vision, and Core Values
3. Philosophy
4. Channels
5. Intended Outcomes
6. Applications and Activities
7. Evaluation

Some of the steps are iterative; influencing and being influenced by other steps in the process. Some steps are unidirectional; influencing adjacent steps but not themselves being influenced. Some steps are permeating; influencing multiple steps of the process while remaining uninfluenced. Each of the steps is described below and placed in an applied context in the next chapter.

The seven steps occur in three stages. Steps 1-3 comprise the first stage in the Intentional Ministry Model. These steps must be addressed in the order in which they appear in the model to assure alignment of the program or ministry to the intentions of the organization as expressed through its mission, vision, core values, and philosophy. It should be noted that Spiritual Engagement is a permeable step that begins at the outset of program or ministry design and continues throughout each step of the process. Stage 2 engages steps 4 and 5 in an iterative conversation with each step influencing the other while remaining wholly under the influence of Spiritual Engagement and governed by Steps 2 and 3 of the process. Stage 3 connects steps 6 and 7 iteratively. Information gained during the Evaluation step (Step 7) influences not only the decisions made during Step 6 but also influences Steps 4 and 5 as evaluation of the program or ministry provides data that lead to altered, replaced, or refined Channels and Intended Outcomes.

Stage 1

Spiritual Engagement

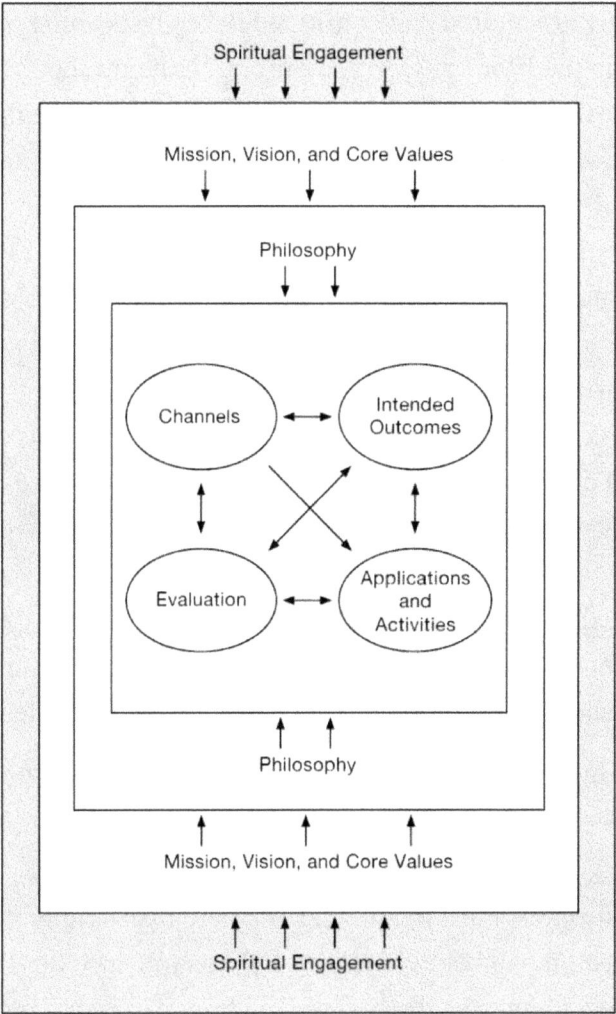

For most if not all Christian organizations, it goes without saying that the Word of God and prayer are central to any decision making by the organization and should permeate all that is done. Being led by God is essential, and this leading is acquired and confirmed through spending quality time in the Word of God and prayer. Numerous books and articles have been written and sermons delivered on the value of reading and meditating upon the Word of God and engaging in fervent prayer. Scripture itself teaches these necessities. Deuteronomy 31:12 entreats the Israelites to hear and follow the words of the law of God. Proverbs 30:15 touts the perfection of God's words. Ephesians 6 identifies the Word of God as the Sword of the Spirit indicating the power it holds. I Timothy 4:5 connects the Word of God and prayer in the context of the goodness of God's creation. Philippians 4:6 encourages believers to make their requests to God through prayer while I Thessalonians 5:17 (NIV) exhorts believers to "pray continually." It should go without saying that the Word of God and prayer are foundational to all Christian endeavors.

It should come as no surprise, then, that the Word of God and prayer form the foundation of the Intentional Ministry Model. Ministry and program design for Christian organizations must be founded on more than simply human intellect; the unbeliever relies solely on intellect, but the believer knows that involving God brings greater depth and allows the process to operate fully in three dimensions (spirit, intellect, and strength) rather than simply the two dimensions of the natural realm (intellect and strength). That is, without seeking the will of God through His Word and through fervent prayer, the design of ministries and programs is relegated to simply a human exercise. However, when the design of a program or ministry is firmly rooted in the Word of God and prayer, the process of designing becomes a spiritual undertaking.

Of significance is that seeking for guidance through the Word of God and prayer is not a one-time event carried out at the beginning of the intentional ministry design process. As the model indicates, engagement with the Word of God and prayer is an ongoing requirement for success in the design of the program or ministry. Note that Jesus encouraged the believers to keep asking, keep seeking, and keep knocking (Matthew 7:7). Paul entreated believers to "pray continually" (I Thessalonians 5:17, NIV). Humans can easily err, and remaining connected to God through prayer and through the reading of His Word helps the design process move ahead with the opportunity to correct errors as they may arise lest they become catastrophic. Simply stated, seeking God's direction throughout the process provides organizational leaders with assurance that God is involved in the process and that they are acting in accordance with His will.

Mission, Vision, and Core Values

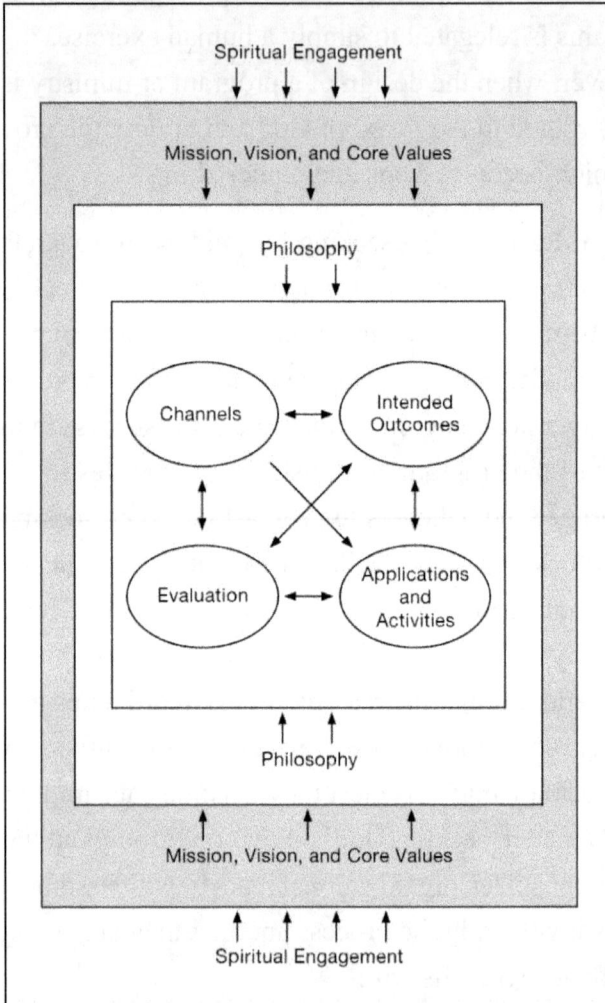

Spiritual Engagement

Mission, Vision, and Core Values

Philosophy

Channels ⟷ Intended Outcomes

Evaluation ⟷ Applications and Activities

Philosophy

Mission, Vision, and Core Values

Spiritual Engagement

Most organizations employ the strategic planning process at some point during their existence. Organizations may engage with strategic planning at the inception of the organization, as a planned evaluation on a regular cycle, during times of growth, or even during times of decline when a new focus may be necessary to refurbish the relevance of the organization and preserve its existence. Depending on when the organization engages with the process, the process may involve a single individual, a small handful of individuals, or a larger collaborative group. In all of these instances, the process requires identification of why the organization exists (mission), how it will fulfill its purpose (vision) and what is of great enough importance to refuse compromise (core values). Together, these ideas keep the organization focused and allow it to move ahead confidently. Indeed, it is from the mission, vision, and core values that the determination is made regarding which programs or ministries the organization should offer.

Mission, vision, and core values are informed by active spiritual engagement. Organizational leaders express their understanding of God's will through clearly stating the mission, vision, and core values of the organization. Once established, these in turn serve the leaders as a guide for future action of the organization. Mission, vision, and core values help filter ideas that arise and allow leaders the opportunity to select those that most closely align to the understood will of God for the organization. Ideas that fall outside of the mission, vision, and core values can be objectively rejected as not aligning to the intentions of the organization while avoiding a personal affront to the individual with the idea. However, continued spiritual engagement remains a necessity as, from time to time, ideas arise that appear outside the mission of the organization but may represent God leading in a new direction to retain the vitality of the organization.

When the leaders of an organization are spiritually engaged and actively seeking God's input through the Word of God and prayer, the intended programs or ministries will be brought into alignment with the mission, vision, and core values. It is critical, then, to understand the mission, vision, and core values of the organization when beginning the process of designing a program or ministry. Notice that the Intentional Ministry Model supports the work done during strategic planning while not being strategic planning itself; intentional design follows and is supported by strategic planning while supporting the strategic plan in return. When enacting the Intentional Ministry Model, then, the mission, vision, and core values drive whether the program or ministry should exist and significantly influence how it will appear and function.

To not align a program or ministry to the mission, vision, and core values of the organization is to assure failure of the program or ministry. The program or ministry will fail either because it is outside the scope of the organization's goals established during strategic planning, because it does not fulfill the purpose of the organization, does not value key ideas of the organization, or places value on worthy ideas that are beyond the manageable scope of the organization. In all of these cases, time spent to consider alignment to the mission, vision, and core values of the organization diminishes the likelihood of failure.

Philosophy of Ministry

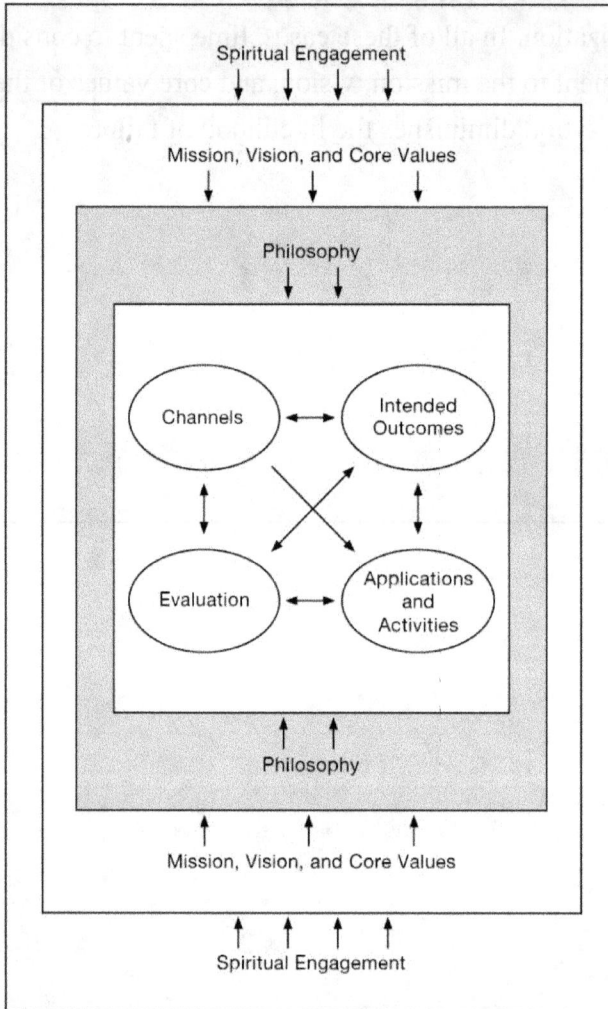

The mission, vision, and core values stem from the organization's philosophy of ministry. However, this relationship is often less than intentional existing purely in the unspoken and unwritten thoughts of organizational leaders. Simply stated, many organizations neglect to consider philosophy of ministry when developing the mission, vision, and core values of the organization. Nonetheless, the philosophical underpinnings of the organization materialize, intentionally or not, through its mission, vision, and core values. Therefore, rather than allow something as significant as philosophy of ministry to emerge randomly and without intent, it is significant that an organization consider its philosophy of ministry.

If philosophy is indeed so significant, why is it not more commonly addressed by organizations and organizational leaders during the development of programs and ministries? There are two root causes to this avoidance of philosophical engagement: time and fear. First, engaging in philosophical consideration and discussion takes time. For many organizations, the need for a new program or ministry is considered urgent and the desire to act quickly drives their actions. Some organizations sidestep the time issue by asserting that they are sure the addition of the new program or ministry is morally and spiritually right which, to their reasoning, negates the need for philosophical consideration. Thus, appropriating time to something so abstract as philosophical engagement, an abstract notion which is often perceived as yielding no tangible result, is not considered by some organizations a luxury to afford. The reality remains, as noted previously, that the philosophy will emerge nonetheless whether by intention or default. Christian leaders, nonetheless, ought not to leave this critical underpinning to chance. If God is in the decision, He has allowed adequate time to plan and act including time to consider the philosophic underpinnings of the organization and their influence on the design of the ministry or program.

Other organizations and organizational leaders shy away from philosophical discussion out of fear. For some, philosophy is an intellectual pursuit to which they do not consider themselves well suited. Indeed, the idea of being a philosopher may even be couched in negative connotation when juxtaposed against images of the likes of well-known philosophers such as Plato or Descartes. Philosophical consideration is undeniably an intellectual pursuit, but it is a pursuit that can be undertaken without becoming a stereotypic philosopher or compromising one's worldview or faith. Philosophical consideration requires the use of tools such as active reflection; disciplined, guided processing; and intention. Grounded in logic and reason, the use of these tools often elicit fear of positioning the organization or leader counter to spiritual leading. However, if one considers Gaebelein's (1985) assertion that God is the source of all truth, then the truth stemming from logic and reason can be seen to emanate from God and is not to be shunned. God has given man the ability to reason.

While one must be cautious to avoid complete reliance on the intellect, logic, and reason of fallen man to the neglect of Godly, spiritual input, there is no need to fear reason or, for that matter, philosophy. Coupled with the wisdom of God and the leading of His Spirit, engagement in philosophical consideration becomes appropriately powerful for the organization and its leadership. This component of the Intentional Ministry Model affirms this concept and provides a means to allow God-given reason and divine leading to flourish together simultaneously and harmoniously.

For others, the need to engage in philosophic consideration is simply a moot point; leaders in this category believe the philosophy of the organization will appear naturally without devoting unnecessary time and effort to the consideration. Unfortunately, what some organizational leaders consider to be naturally arising philosophy is in reality accidental philosophy. Rather, the philosophy of an organization should emerge from intentional, meaningful discussion among stakeholders. It should not be left to chance under the guise of being a natural emergence of the organization's philosophy. Simply stated, organic and accidental are two distinctly different notions.

Stage 2

Channels of Ministry and Intended Outcomes

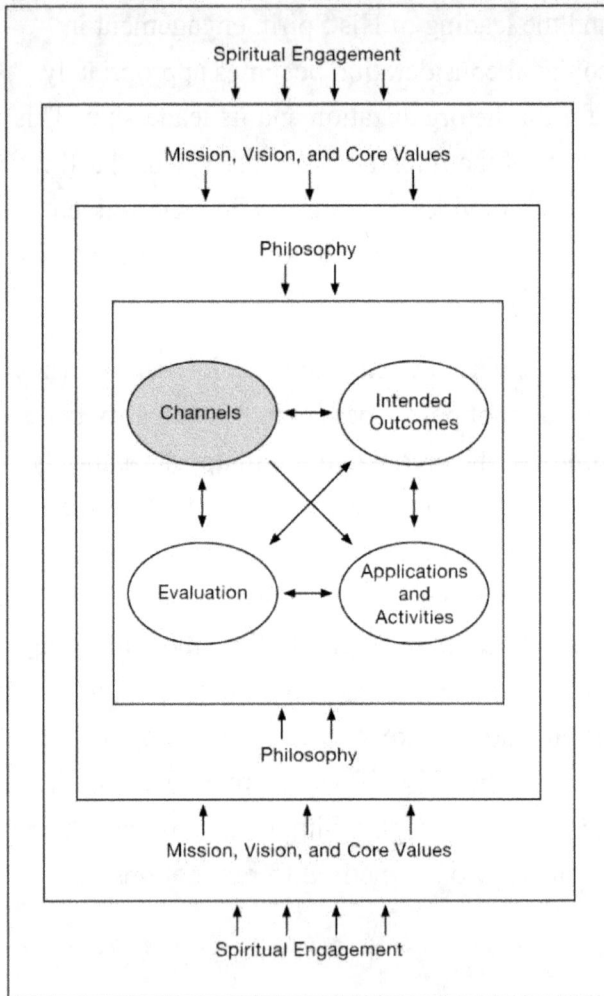

With a spiritual foundation securely laid and the mission, vision, values and philosophy of the organization firmly established and overtly stated, consideration turns to the more practical aspects of designing programs and ministries. Indeed, this is the place where most organizational leaders tend to prefer to begin the planning process, bypassing the abstract mission, vision, core values, and philosophy stages in favor of the concrete notion of what to do. In light of the mission, vision, and values of the organization, the question is now raised regarding what God is speaking into the hearts of leaders to accomplish by instituting this new program or ministry. This is an exciting part of the process as this is where the God-given vision and idea begin to come to life as the form of a program or ministry emerges. Nonetheless, this segment of the process can be frustrating to organizational leaders who have spent a seemingly endless span of time in the abstract ideas of mission, vision, core values, and philosophy and are ready to immerse themselves in the planning of events, activities, and tasks that are the visible, actionable face of the program or ministry.

However, intentionality in the design of programs and ministries takes time, effort, and thought. While this critical stage of the process becomes significantly more concrete than the previous stages, it remains the development of a largely invisible but critically necessary infrastructure. Thus, some organizational leaders feel mired in the world of abstraction craving practicality but not finding as much of it as they desire at the moment. To those leaders is the plea to continue through the process as practicality is certainly on the horizon. Indeed, it is hoped that leaders will embrace this part of the process and revel in the creative expression of the God-given vision.

This stage of the process involves two related steps that engage with one another in an iterative conversation with each step influencing the other while remaining wholly under the influence of Spiritual Engagement and governed by the mission, vision, values, and philosophy established earlier in the process. The first is to ask the question, "What should participants in this program or ministry know and be able to do as a result of engaging with the program or ministry?" In other words, it is during this stage that the intended outcomes (goals) of the program or ministry become tangible. The second is to group similar goals together into larger categories (channels of ministry) as a means of providing structure to the ideas; the full purpose of developing channels of ministry will be discussed shortly.

The process of answering the question, "What should participants in this program or ministry know and be able to do as a result of engaging with the program or ministry?" commences as a significant brainstorming exercise. To allow time for individuals to prepare and consider, the question is presented to project participants a few days prior to the brainstorming session. When the project participants are assembled, then, the question is posed to the group, and the brainstorming of ideas begins. No answers are ignored, and no judgment regarding the worth of an answer is passed at this point. A certain amount of redundancy is expected in this part of the process. Nonetheless, all ideas are captured and made visible to the entire group. Some use traditional methods such as white boards, chart paper, or even sticky notes while more technologically-savvy groups may capture ideas in a document or electronic collaborative space. The tools employed are not of any consequence. It is simply important that the ideas are readily visible to the group for consideration and that each idea is captured as a discrete item that can be easily moved as the channel structure is applied after the brainstorming is complete. The brainstorming process ends when new information ceases to come forth. In practical terms, this is a meeting that should be scheduled with plenty of time available. Since interrupting brainstorming is not usually a wise idea as it curtails creativity, participants should plan to meet for as long as necessary to complete the brainstorming. Once the initial brainstorming is complete, it is reasonable to adjourn the meeting and to commence the next session by asking if any additional ideas have surfaced in the interim. These new ideas are gathered and made visible along with the plethora of thoughts from the initial brainstorming session. Specific examples of brainstormed lists appear in chapters 4 and 5.

Once assured that no additional ideas are forthcoming, the project participants are now tasked with grouping the ideas into categories of similar ideas called channels of ministry. This is why it is important to have each idea captured as a discrete piece of data that can be easily moved from one location to another. Hence, sticky notes or electronic tools are recommended. The purpose of grouping ideas into channels of ministry is to provide additional structure that leaders can use in planning events and activities that will meet the intended outcomes of the program. For example, most programs or ministries will have 3-6 channels of ministry. So, a program or ministry having four channels could focus on meeting the intended outcomes of one of those channels each quarter of the year. Some goals are meaningfully addressed concurrently, and having the broader channels can bring those to light. Further, channels of ministry provide program or ministry leaders with a few simply-identified segments of the program or ministry that are easily evaluated to assure each is being addressed during routine operation of the program or ministry. Coupling channels with the assessment component of the Model allows for adjustments to operations to be made with reasoned intent rather than guesswork based in anecdotal information. The ultimate goal of the Intentional Ministry Model is to assure that the program or ministry remains focused on what God has called the organization to do and to be able to account for it being done.

Practically, the question that guides this part of the process is, "Which of the goals (intended outcomes) in the massive list are similar and could be grouped together?" As the grouping process begins, nothing is deleted. If ideas seem redundant, place them in close proximity to one another, but be sure that the idea is seen as having emerged multiple times. Create new groups as necessary; if a goal does not fit in an existing group, create a new one. As the characteristics of each group appear, name the group. For example, in the Boomer ministry that will be described later, one of the channels was *Connect* and contained goals that related to enhancing social interactions as members of the Body of Christ. As the initial sorting is completed, consider the number of channels. A good target is to have 3-6 channels. Have the group prayerfully consider whether two or more of the groups could merge into one broader channel. Also have the group consider if there is an aspect of the program or ministry that is not represented by the channels that have been created; create a new channel if necessary. Specific examples of channels appear in chapters 4 and 5.

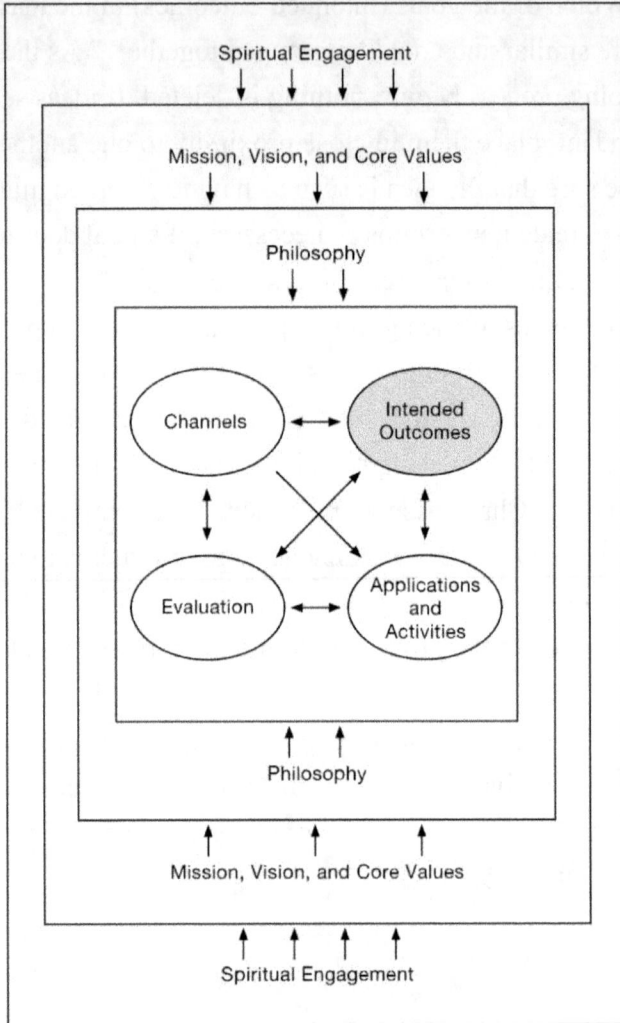

With the rough ideas of goals now grouped into named channels of ministry, it is time to refine the goals into measurable intended outcomes. Consider that each goal should be an imperative statement beginning with an action verb. For example, a worship ministry might have an outcome to "Differentiate worship ministry from concert-style performance." Educators use the taxonomy developed by Bloom, Engelhart, Furst, Hill, & Krathwohl (1956) to help structure goals at various levels of complexity, and it is reasonable to apply that concept to intended outcomes of a program or ministry. Hence, having a project participant or engaging a consultant with a background in education and/or curricular design is helpful here as this is often not a common task for the average business person or vocational minister while it may be more familiar to a professional educator.

The refinement process will be an iterative process that requires a reasonable amount of time to complete. It is suggested that drafts of the intended outcomes be written in the project meeting one week and reviewed as a group in the meeting of the next week with each individual project participant prayerfully considering the drafted outcomes and coming to the meeting with improvement suggestions. The group then considers the notes of the participants and adjusts the statements of the intended outcomes accordingly. While it is reasonable to expect conversations around one or more of the intended outcomes to require significant thought and refining work, it is important not to let the revision meeting get out of hand with the conversation following extraneous paths of thought. A strong project manager/facilitator helps to keep the group focused and to guide them to conclusive decisions regarding the intended outcomes. Ideally, all participants should leave the refinement session having approved all or very nearly all of the intended outcomes. If additional time and consideration are needed or meeting duration is limited because of scheduling constraints, it is reasonable to schedule one or more additional sessions to complete the drafting and refining process. The important thing to keep in mind is that the process, while iterative, is not endless. Participants should be aware that initial decisions on outcomes must be made in a reasonable amount of time. It is also important to note that the organization is not eternally obligated to these outcomes if the need or intention changes in the future. Indeed, the Intentional Ministry Model requires that programs and their intended outcomes be reviewed periodically to assure that the program is still meeting the needs of its participants and staying abreast of current trends and information. Specific examples of intended outcomes appear in chapters 4 and 5.

Ultimately, the channels and outcomes serve as an operations guide for program or ministry leaders who should refer to the channels and outcomes to determine what has been done and what needs to be done in the course of operating the ministry. While closely related to the assessment component of the model, this application of channels and outcomes is an initial and ongoing application as leaders use the channels and outcomes as a planning tool for the program or ministry. Recall that by nature and unlike the traditional education setting with specific grade levels that participants complete, programs and ministries often have no tangible conclusion; they continue indefinitely. So leaders should consider addressing channels and outcomes on a cyclical basis. While care should be taken not to address one outcome to the neglect of others (that is, after all, a significant reason for engaging in program or ministry design in the first place), it is reasonable that an outcome is addressed multiple times in a cycle. Indeed, this pattern of introduction, reinforcement, and assessment is theoretically sound. Thus, fully employing the channels and outcomes allows program and ministry leaders to rest assured that all aspects of the program or ministry are addressed periodically.

Ministry Applications and Activities

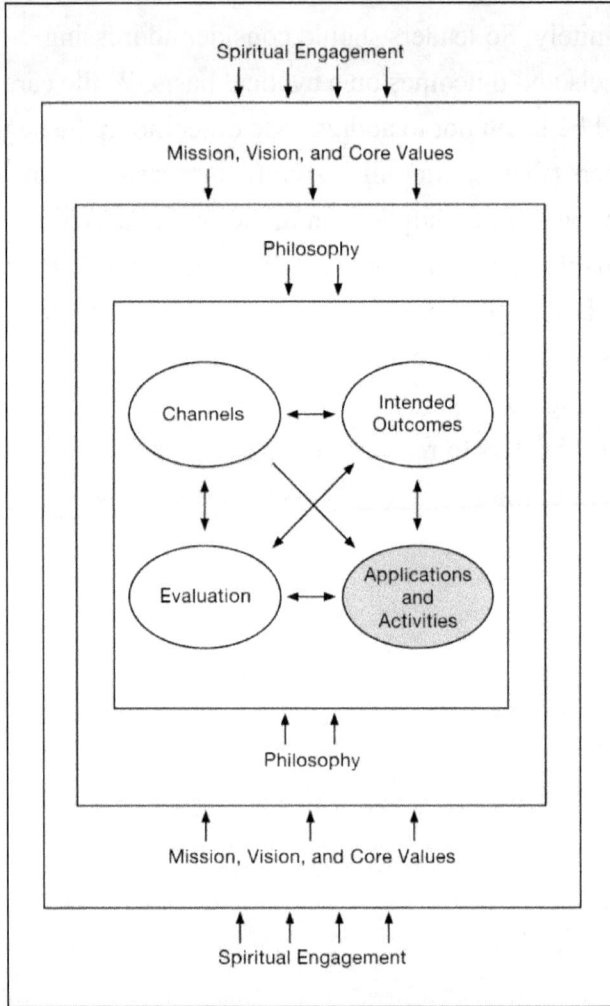

Spiritual Engagement

Mission, Vision, and Core Values

Philosophy

Channels ⟷ Intended Outcomes

Evaluation ⟷ Applications and Activities

Philosophy

Mission, Vision, and Core Values

Spiritual Engagement

At long last, there is rejoicing for the practically minded individuals who have so patiently waded through the mire of abstraction and foundation creation as this part of the model now addresses the question with which many leaders wish to begin the design process: "What are the tangible activities we going to do in this program or ministry?" However, because of the design process, the project participants now have a means to engage in focused conversation regarding the activities of the program or ministry.

The discussion is a brainstorming session similar to that used to initially uncover the outcomes and channels of ministry. This session focuses on each of the program outcomes identified earlier. To do this, the project manager/facilitator raises the question, "How will we <insert outcome here>?" It is wise as well as courteous to make participants aware of this question at the end of the previous meeting and again in the interim via electronic, verbal, or other communication to allow participants time to consider creative ways to accomplish the ministry goals.

As with the initial brainstorming session to determine program outcomes, no answers are ignored, and no judgment regarding the worth of an answer is passed at this point. A certain amount of redundancy is expected in this part of the process as in the brainstorming of potential outcomes. All ideas are captured and made visible to the entire group. As in the previous brainstorming session, use of traditional methods such as white boards, chart paper, or even sticky notes or the capturing of ideas in a document or electronic collaborative space is important so the ideas are readily visible to the group for consideration and so each idea is captured as a discrete item that can be easily moved. As previously, the brainstorming process ends when new information ceases to come forth. In practical terms, this is a meeting that should be scheduled with plenty of time available. Since interrupting brainstorming is not usually a wise idea as it curtails creativity, participants should plan to meet for as long as necessary to complete the brainstorming. Once the initial brainstorming is complete, it is reasonable to adjourn the meeting and to commence the next session by asking if any additional ideas have surfaced in the interim. These new ideas are gathered and made visible along with the plethora of thoughts from the initial brainstorming session.

From here, there task becomes determining which activities are the best application of the ministry outcomes. This involves consideration of such things as the budget, stakeholder personalities, and available physical resources. It is common for the project participants to complete the brainstorming of initial ideas and then to delegate the selection of activities to the individual responsible for discharging the program or ministry. Nonetheless, project participants can offer program or ministry leaders some reasonable direction before fully delegating the operations. For example, the determination of whether a so-called "chips and salsa event" is worthwhile is a realistic conversation for this group. In the Boomer ministry that will be described later, one of the channels was *Connect* and contained goals that related to enhancing social interactions as members of the Body of Christ. So, while the entirety of the ministry did not revolve around "chips and salsa events," there was clearly a meaningful place for such events in the purview of the ministry. Having established clear channels and outcomes made this a simple conversation for the project participants and prevented opinion-based conflict as this type of event was already meaningfully integrated into the design of the ministry.

Because the applications and activities arise from the goal of meeting ministry outcomes, it should become relatively simple to plan meaningful activities and to provide program/ministry participants a sense of purpose surrounding those activities. This shared sense of purpose communicated clearly to participants has the potential to serve as a unifying factor improving group identity and cohesion as participants rally around the shared purposes of the activities and connect them to the greater context of fulfilling program or ministry goals.

Stage 3

Ministry/Program Evaluation

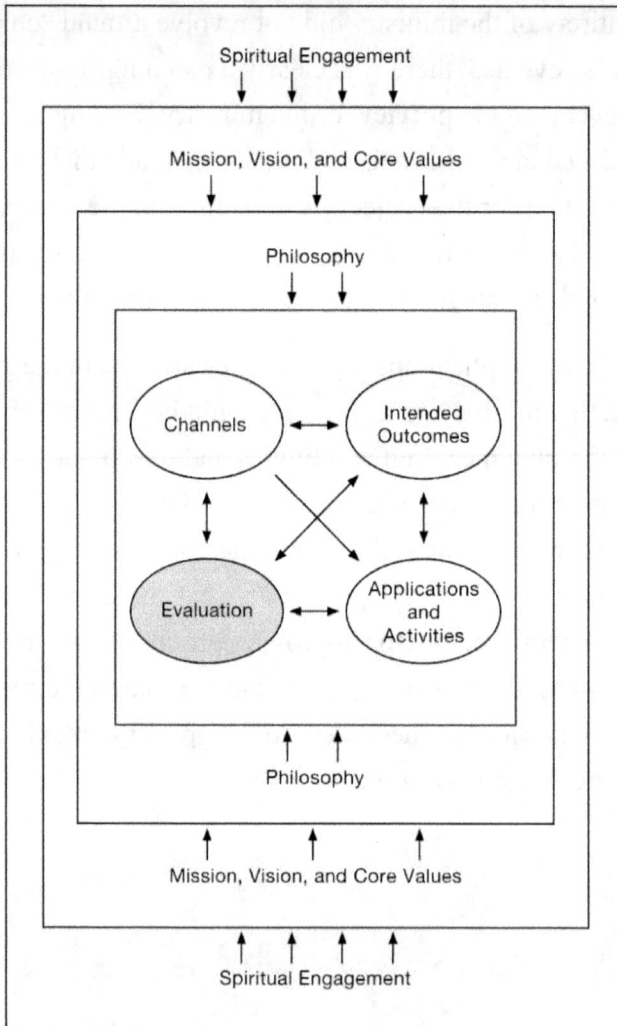

The notion of evaluating a ministry or a program is, for some, a source of deep angst. In many, though certainly not all, church and parachurch organizations, systematic evaluation of ministries or programs is non-existent. Some leaders simply do not consider it necessary to evaluate ministries or programs. The unstated reason is often that the organization was directed by God to enter into the ministry or program, so it will continue to operate the ministry or program until such time as God directs otherwise. Evaluation is simply not necessary. Other leaders avoid evaluation using the same unstated reasoning above, but the reasoning is founded in an underlying notion that they are unworthy to evaluate a ministry or program that God instituted in their midst and of which they are merely stewards. Evaluation is simply not proper. For these leaders, it is important to establish program and ministry evaluation as a viable part of the ministry design process and to clarify the method and purpose of program and ministry evaluation.

For some organizations, the evaluation of a ministry or program raises questions related to what happens if the evaluation of the ministry or program is not favorable. In Christian circles, placing blame for failure is rightfully avoided in favor of extending grace, showing compassion, and reflecting a Christ-like attitude. However, some organizations grasp these virtues to the detriment of honesty and continue programs or ministries that are ineffective, misaligned to the organization, or simply not necessary for one reason or another. Having developed into the design of the program or ministry clearly established intended outcomes and both formative and summative assessment measures that allow on-the-fly adjustments and long-range evaluation, respectively, intentional design creates an objective stance that allows organizations to review programs or ministries as unique entities in and of themselves rather than as emotional appendages of individuals. Further, intentional design actually reduces the chance of the program or ministry failing because of the objective formative assessments that allow for quick midstream adjustments to the program or ministry without completely abandoning the program or ministry in favor of the latest fad masquerading as a new idea.

Related to this is the concern of what happens when the program or ministry undergoes planned summative (long-term) evaluation and is found ineffective, misaligned, or unnecessary. The Intentional Ministry Model addresses this well as the decision to either discontinue or completely revise a program or ministry becomes fully objective. The results of the evaluation indicate whether the program or ministry is meeting the established outcomes. If not, leaders are able to use the data gathered to objectively determine whether to significantly revise the design of the ministry (including adapting or replacing ministry activities) or to discontinue it. The need to continue in prayer and seeking to hear the voice of God are evident as leaders seek to make data-based decisions but must not neglect the spiritual aspect of ministry. For example, if the evaluation reveals that the goals of the ministry or program are not being met but leaders believe the calling remains to operate the program or ministry, the evaluation data can show where to make active adjustments to meet the goals of the program or ministry or, if necessary, to adjust the goals of the program or ministry to align with its demonstrated outcomes.

Two types of evaluation are used in assessing programs and ministries developed using the Intentional Ministry Model: formative (short-term) and summative (long-term). Formative evaluation is often, though not always, more informal than summative evaluation. Since formative evaluation can be conceptualized as a quick "temperature check" of the program for the purpose of making minor course corrections as needed, it often uses anecdotal data with, perhaps, some basic descriptive data such as numbers of participants or individuals served. It can be used to make minor corrections or adaptations, but formative evaluation should not be used to determine whether to continue a program or ministry. Such a determination requires the deeper, long-term focus of summative evaluation. Summative evaluation commonly involves gathering of significant amounts of data from a variety of sources. It takes time, but it is doable and worth the effort.

In practice, program or ministry evaluation stems from the established outcomes developed using the Intentional

Ministry Model. The evaluation process begins by asking the question, "Are the intended outcomes being met?" From that simple question come the follow-up notions of, "If so, how well? If not, why not?" and, whether the program or ministry is successful or not, "How can we improve?" The answers to these questions come from deliberately gathered data about the ministry. This data comes from documented records such as worship service attendance numbers, recorded conversions to the faith, or numbers of families served by a food distribution network. All of this is objective data. However, in terms of program or ministry success at meeting outcomes, it may be difficult to quantify the data; numbers alone may be inadequate. So, program or ministry leaders may need to conduct planned interviews with participants to determine if they perceive of the program or ministry as successful, what they like about the program or ministry, and what they might like to see changed going forward. They may also need to gather other anecdotal data or ask additional questions through a survey. If using survey data, it is wise to enlist the assistance of an individual with research or educational experience who can help formulate survey questions that will garner the right type of information.

Once the data is gathered, program or ministry leaders need to convene a collaborative group to assist in the interpretation of the results. The Intentional Ministry Model is a collaborative model; it requires multiple inputs from multiple sources to assure maximum effectiveness.

Therefore, leaders should assemble a group of core individuals who will serve throughout the evaluation process. These individuals should represent the varied stakeholder groups within the church or organization. Participants should be chosen who have a vested interest in the ministry or program, who oversee or participate in complementary ministries or programs, or who simply have a passion for ministry and a heart to engage in the process. In addition, it is wise to have at least one project participant who is familiar with program evaluation as used in the Intentional Ministry Model or a similar setting. This individual should serve as the project manager or project facilitator whether that service is paid or voluntary. He or she should be familiar with basic statistics and/or qualitative research methods. In situations where an experienced program evaluation individual is not readily available among the stakeholders, it makes sense to secure the services of an external consultant who has familiarity with program or ministry evaluation and who will serve as the project manager/facilitator.

Once this group is assembled, the intentional review of the program or ministry continues by examining the intended outcomes and asking if those outcomes are being met. There should be few or no surprises here either for leaders or other stakeholders since the outcomes of the program or ministry were clearly established, ongoing formative evaluation has been occurring, and the means of conducting summative evaluation of whether the outcomes are being met was pre-determined. The evaluation process should also be non-threatening to stakeholders as its purpose is to celebrate what is being done well and make improvements to what is not working properly such as planning a means to address outcomes that are not being met. If a significant number of outcomes are not being met, stakeholders now use the objective data gained in conjunction with significant prayer and seeking the Lord to determine whether to revise or discontinue the program or ministry. If outcomes are not being met, a deeper inspection of the data should help reveal the source of the deficiency and afford leaders and stakeholders an opportunity for frank yet objective discussion of available options. This conversation may become unpleasant, but if leaders can remain objective and focused on facts rather than on individuals and emotions, an awkward situation can become more manageable. It is important to be honest but objective and to avoid placing blame on an individual or group. By speaking in terms of expected outcomes and the relevant data, leaders and stakeholders can more easily discuss possibilities to move the organization forward.

If the data indicate that a significant number of outcomes are not being met, the outcomes may be incorrect or may have become invalid as the program or ministry has progressed. This is not to be taken as a negative situation; there is no blame to place on the program/ministry design or on those who enact the program or ministry. Things change, and that is alright. In some cases, it may be necessary to revise the program/ministry design to accommodate for new outcomes or to replace those that are not working or have become outmoded. This is actually a key purpose of the evaluation portion of the Intentional Ministry Model as it allows the ministry or program to change as necessary and for intended outcomes to be revised in keeping with the established purposes of the program or ministry.

Before determining to discontinue a program or ministry, leaders and other stakeholders should prayerfully consider the available options for revision and closely examine the gathered data. If the decision remains that the best option is to discontinue the program or ministry, the rationale should be based on the gathered data and the determination made without placing blame on the program or ministry leader or the volunteers or staff serving in the program or ministry. This is not to say that discussions should not be frank and honest or that the truth should not be stated in love as Paul writes to the Ephesians (Ephesians 4:15). However, the "in love" must not be overlooked; there are still human beings created in the image of God who are involved in the program or ministry and who will be affected by the decision rendered.

The evaluation of a program or ministry is not a one-time event upon which the very life or death of the program or ministry hangs. Formative (short-term) evaluation should be routinely conducted. For example, gathering data about the success of an application of the program or ministry (special event, class, session, etc.) should be routinely gathered. Even simple anecdotal data gathered from a handful of participants exiting a class or special event will provide reasonable information to begin identifying actions that should be continued or discontinued. Remember, though, that an adjustment to an application of ministry should never be made on the basis of one individual piece of data. Just as guilt or innocence should be determined by two or three witnesses (2 Corinthians 13:1), so ministry decisions should consider multiple inputs. These inputs should be used to make ongoing adjustments and may also be saved as qualitative data for future summative (long-term) assessment. Summative assessment should be conducted on a planned and consistent schedule. Typically, summative evaluation is conducted during every third year that a program or ministry operates. Summative evaluation is a longer process than formative (short-term) evaluation. So, leaders should plan accordingly so the evaluation is completed by the end of every third year of operation. That is not to say that summative evaluation cannot be conducted more frequently. However, while circumstances may impose, it is not recommended to delay a summative evaluation cycle beyond every third year of operation. This requires leaders to commit to the evaluation process including devoting time and resources to gather and analyze data. However, it is an essential component of the Intentional Ministry Model.

Part 2: Applications

While having a theoretical understanding of a model or process is valuable, it often helps to see the merit of the model by examining its application in a variety of situations. To that end, two ministries that were developed using the model are described in the following chapters. Notice that while the development process for each ministry was the same, the results were unique based on the needs of the ministry and its leaders and participants.

Chapter 4:

Adult Teaching Ministry

Background

A medium-sized church convened a committee to review the Adult Teaching Ministry of the church. Thus, the project participant selection step of the model was accomplished by ministry leaders. What emerged quickly in the initial meeting and conversation with the participants was that there was no discernible structure to the Adult Teaching Ministry within the church. Ministry leaders expressed frustration at the lack of stable direction and multiple failed attempts to simply insert a new program to fix the problem rather than consider the long-term needs of the congregation. What was needed was a reasonable structure that could guide the Adult Teaching Ministry and circumvent the church's traditional practice of approaching potential teachers at the last-minute to ask what they might want to teach in the new quarter. This practice had led to a haphazard approach to adult teaching and subsequently to a ministry fraught with both redundancies and gaps in information. The leadership of the church recognized this and was searching for a means to develop a guiding framework for the ministry that could reasonably be used for many years to come and would eliminate gaps and redundancies while remaining easily adaptable as change necessitated. Some current teachers remained concerned, though, with regard to the fate of their particular course or teaching platform within the church; would those be retained after all the time and effort to build solid ministries? After nearly an hour of bemoaning past failures and time wasted, questioning whether a solution actually existed, and coming to grips with somewhat territorial concerns, the participants seemingly unanimously sought more information about the solution alluded to earlier in the meeting – the Intentional Ministry Model.

At this point, the infinite and qualitative nature of the Adult Teaching Ministry surfaced. It became clear that many participants had been involved in aspects of this ministry for many years and were desirous of continuing to be involved. It was also clear that this was not a program that would be well suited to traditional quantitative evaluation methods; participants loved their groups and were emotionally connected to them. So, measuring success of these groups would need an entirely different approach.

Assembling the Participants

The Intentional Ministry Model is a collaborative model; it requires multiple inputs from multiple sources to assure maximum effectiveness. Participants should be chosen who have a vested interest in the ministry or program, who oversee or participate in complementary ministries or programs, or who simply have a passion for ministry and a heart to engage in the process. In addition, it is wise to appoint a project manager/facilitator who is familiar with the Intentional Ministry Model or who has experience in ministry, program, or even curriculum design. The commitment required may be for a few months or, in some extreme cases, up to a year or more.

As noted above, the project participants had already been carefully selected from a broad spectrum of stakeholders. So, expertise was abounding. Project participants included past and present teachers of adult classes, pastoral leaders, and other educational experts. Given the events described above, it was a seemingly natural appointment for the individual with curriculum design experience to assume the role of project manager/facilitator.

In the Intentional Ministry Model, content creation participants are collectively responsible for the creation of program content. These individuals must be able to reason well and to bring creative ideas to the group for consideration and critical review. They must be able to disconnect emotionally as needed in order to critically appraise their own ideas and the ideas of others without becoming offended, yet they must remain passionate about the development of the program and willing to defend ideas that are challenged when such defense is merited. To accomplish this required allowing project participants to freely express concerns over past failures and time wasted and to question how this process would be any different. Once they concluded that the model would create a meaningful and adaptable framework for the ministry, they readily committed to the process that, unknown at the time, would last nearly a year because of the volume of work to be done and the frequent interruptions to the meeting schedule. The church provided an online forum for participants to interact between meetings. This forum was instrumental in keeping the process moving and the goal in sight over the long period of development.

The Intentional Ministry Model

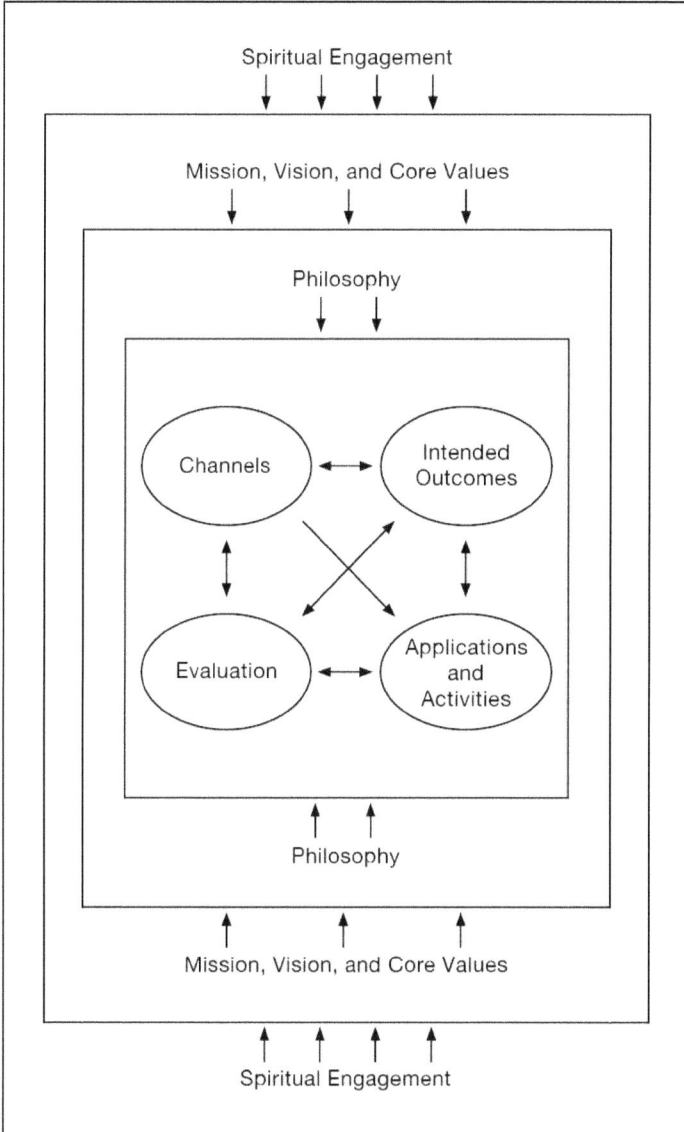

Stage 1

Spiritual Engagement

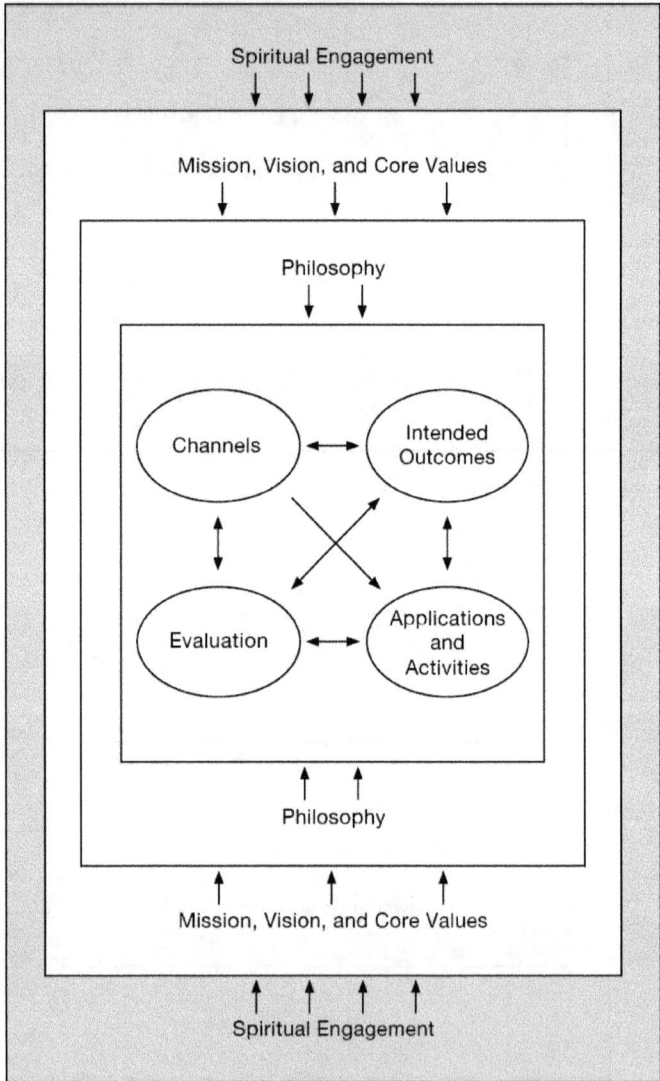

Spiritual Engagement

Mission, Vision, and Core Values

Philosophy

Channels ⟷ Intended Outcomes

Evaluation ⟷ Applications and Activities

Philosophy

Mission, Vision, and Core Values

Spiritual Engagement

Spiritual engagement was relatively simple for his group of project participants. Each had a vested interest in the success of the project, and each carried a distinct call to ministry. So, prayer, searching the Word of God, and other spiritual activities came naturally. All of the participants had a sense of the deep responsibility to correctly teach the orthodox Word of Truth as entreated by Paul in 2 Timothy 2:15. Even as the process extended into weeks and months, prayer continued steadily. The participants were engaged spiritually throughout the process.

Mission, Vision, and Core Values

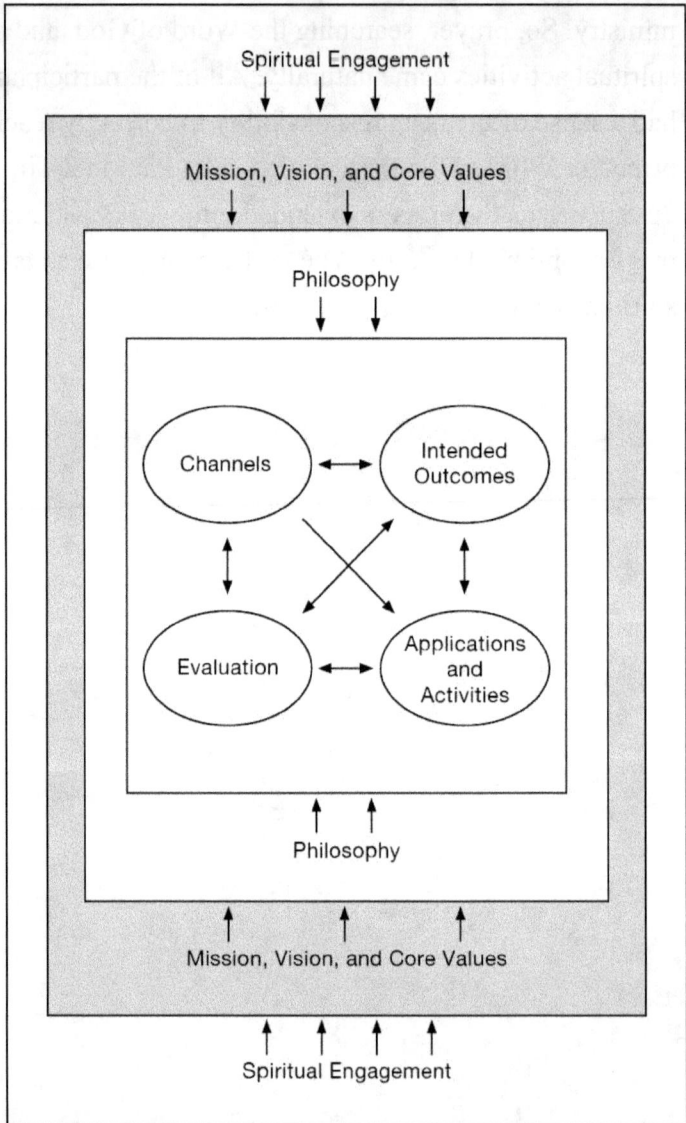

While the church had statements of mission, vision, and core values, they were largely dysfunctional. The church would, over the next two years, embark on a collaborative project to revise these expressions, but the adult teaching project was to be completed prior. So, the project participants gleaned the general intention of the existing mission and a transitional vision statement put forth by church leaders, and they identified core values that, while not the "official" listing of the church, were believed to align with those statements so that the design process could move forward.

Existing Mission Statement

To lead people of all ages into a life changing relationship with Jesus

---

Transitional Vision Statement

Connect. Grow. Serve.

Teacher-Created List of Core Values
Relationships
Academic Integrity
Comprehensive Understanding
Authenticity
Sound Doctrine
Diversity
Expository Teaching

Philosophy of Ministry

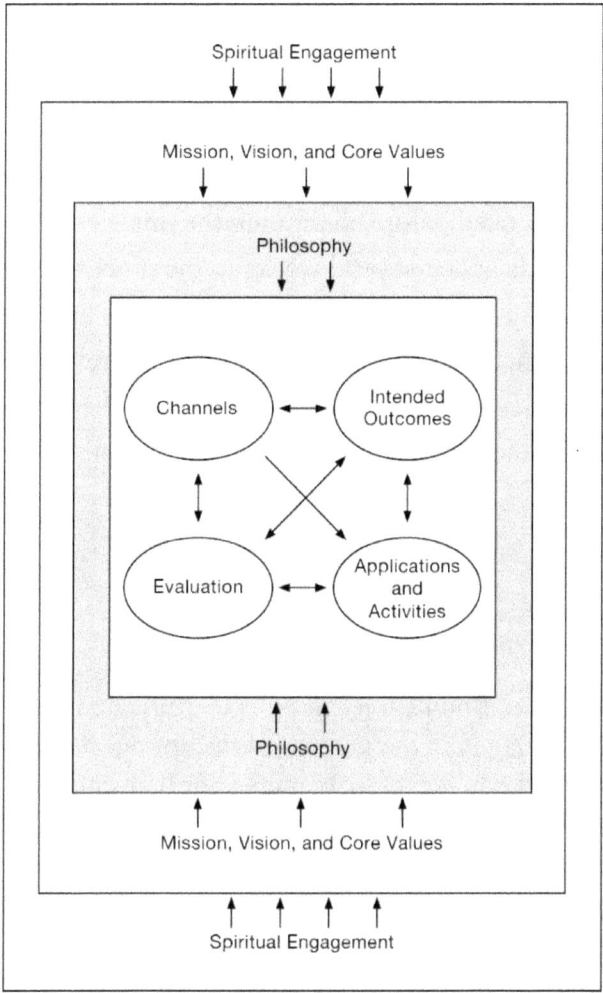

As the discussion turned to philosophy of ministry, it was quickly noted that this had never been a topic of discussion and particularly not in the context of adult teaching where philosophy of ministry and philosophy of education were mingled. Being committed to the entirety of the process and seeing the necessity of a well-articulated and sound philosophy of ministry, the project participants elected to address this need before continuing the ministry design process. This added several weeks to the process, but the end result was a solid philosophy on which to build the ministry. That philosophy is adapted and abbreviated below. Notice how the philosophy connects the core values along with the mission and vision of the organization.

Teaching Philosophy

Purpose of Biblical Teaching

The purpose of biblical teaching is to cultivate individuals who are engaged in the process of becoming lifelong learners and who develop an increasingly insatiable desire to grow in their knowledge of God through His Word. Biblical teaching guides learners to be discerning of sound doctrine and to adopt a Christ-centered worldview. Biblical teaching supports learners as they pursue lives of authenticity that are characterized by healthy relationships, repentance, and the freedom to be real and vulnerable all while maintaining points of tangency with the culture around them yet without having their faith diluted by or yielding to ungodly thinking.

Nature of the Learner

We recognize the teaching that, due to man's corrupted human nature, the disciplines of spiritual formation are needed to train the will and to build redeeming character, behavior, and habits in the learner. The Church will attempt to reach and teach each individual where he or she is spiritually, intellectually, physically, and emotionally. We seek to deliver an educational program that allows participants to enhance their knowledge, skills, and spiritual gifts in a variety of ways. We recognize the social nature of man and attempt to connect individuals socially and spiritually in order to foster spiritual growth leading to sustained service.

Nature of the Teaching/Learning Process

The teaching/learning process brings into play an interaction of various contexts (church, family, and community) that encourage the learner's spiritual formation. The learner presents a spiritual standing, a set of prior knowledge, an intellectual capacity, a style of learning and motivation, both internal and external. The teacher brings a set of knowledge, skills, and competencies, which are implemented through prayer, planning, management, and instruction that engage and uplift the learner. The teacher/learner relationship fosters the interconnectedness that is characteristic of the Body of Christ. Teachers grasp teachable moments to disciple and encourage learners in their spiritual formation so that the Body of Christ is edified.

Role of the Teacher

First of all, according to the Scripture not everyone should teach (James 3:1). Just because someone desires to teach doesn't mean he/she is qualified to do so. There is a weight and a burden to teaching, and a teacher should realize the tremendous responsibility that is upon him or her. The role of the teacher is a vital role in the church, and a teacher of God's Word should be Gospel-driven and Christ-centered, discerning, deliberate, faithful in service, holistic, motivating, and a maker of disciples.

Educational Role of the Local Church

Since the Scriptures teach that education is the responsibility of believers and the Church (Matthew 28:20), our church envisions serving people by coming alongside them to build relationships that connect the individual to the Church and encourage them to grow spiritually toward engagement in sustained service. It is, therefore, the intent of our church to present learners with education developed from a Christian worldview and sound doctrine using sound and consistent hermeneutical principles to interpret the author's intent of Scripture.

Stage 2

Channels of Ministry and Intended Outcomes

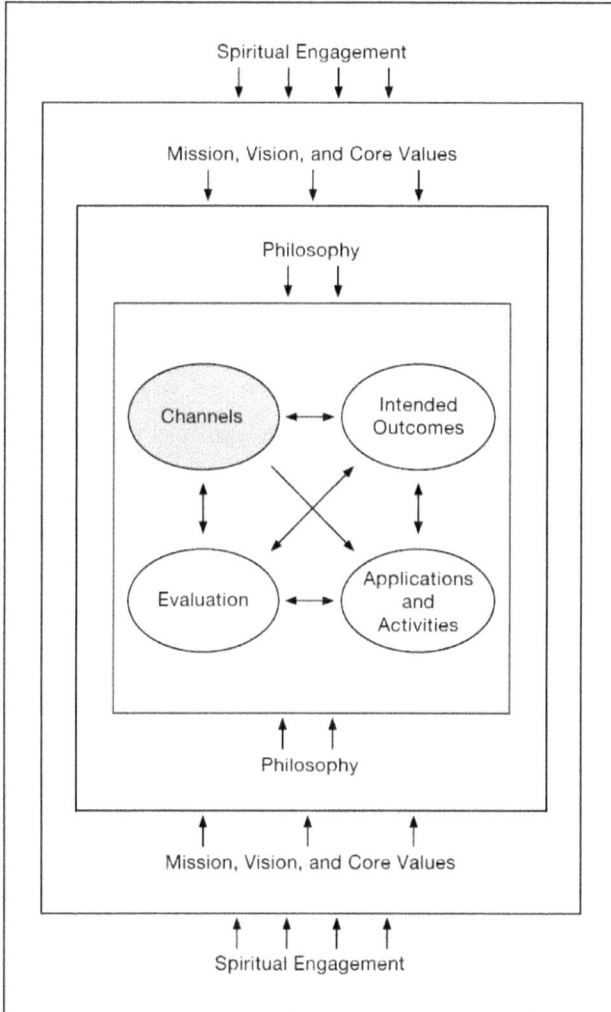

Once the philosophy of ministry was developed, the project participants confidently turned to the task of determining what participants should know and be able to do as a result of participating in the Adult Teaching Ministry. At this point, the notion of an infinite ministry serving congregants for potentially many years surfaced clearly. Project participants had to grapple with the concept that, unlike educational programs for grade school or high school, there was no "graduation" to the next group; all ages from young adults through senior citizens were under the umbrella of the Adult Teaching Ministry. While each group would certainly have unique needs, the Adult Teaching Ministry, through its mission, vision, core values, and philosophy had established a clear commitment to address the educational needs of adults as a whole rather than fragmenting this segment of the population. Thus, the infinite nature of the ministry exerted a significant influence on the intended outcomes that were developed.

The project participants began by brainstorming what they wanted adults to know and be able to do (knowledge and skills) as a result of interacting with (notice that the notion was not that of *completing*) the Adult Teaching Ministry. That list is below. No idea was discarded, and no judgments passed on ideas at this point. The purpose was simply to capture all of the ideas for future evaluation and classification. If an idea sounded familiar to one already mentioned, the participants paused to consider if the ideas were the same or if there were subtle differences between them. In either case, the idea was captured by a new item in the list or as a marking indicating the duplication. As an aside here, duplication can be a signal of two things: it can either indicate that the idea is significant enough to be mentioned multiple times and needs to be given the due attention, or it can signify that the brainstorming is coming to a close. When one meeting was clearly not going to be enough time to complete the brainstorming, the project participants agreed to continue meeting on a weekly basis to complete the project.

Partial List of Brainstormed Knowledge and Skills

Adult Teaching Ministry

Spiritual formation
Sound doctrine
Worldview
Baptism and Lord's Supper
Biblical history
Meta-narrative of Scripture
Tenets of orthodox theology
Exegesis
Holy Spirit
Connect Old Testament and New Testament
Loci of theology
Personal testimony of conversion
Spiritual disciplines
The Bible and life
Living out the Christian life
Evangelism
Spiritual gifts/giftedness
Learning to lead

Brainstormed Knowledge and Skills (cont.)
Biblical view of leadership Mentoring Community outreach

As the facilitator began to notice a longer lag between the offering of ideas from the participants and significant duplication of ideas, the participants were queried regarding whether they believed they had exhausted all of the ideas. Once each of the participants indicated an end to personal contributions, the brainstorming session drew to a conclusion. It should be noted here that this session ending did not preclude participants from adding to the list at a later time. Indeed, with some time away from the flurry of group activity, some participants returned with additional ideas to consider; these were received and added to the list to await the impending classification and validation that the model requires of all brainstormed ideas.

The brainstorming concluded, participants were asked to begin grouping ideas into sets of similar themes. The use of "sticky notes" helped facilitate this process as brainstormed ideas placed one per note were readily able to be moved by participants. Electronic tools are also available to facilitate this process. Categories were named once enough items were placed in each group to demonstrate its theme. Categories continued to be created as each idea was considered and those that did not seem to fit the existing categories were set aside until other related ideas surfaced and defined the nature of the set as differing from the existing categories. The categorization process took one full meeting session.

Once each and every brainstormed idea was placed in a category, the participants were asked to begin the next session by considering if any of the categories could be combined. Next, participants were asked to consider if, in light of the existing categories, there were any that might be missing or if any of the brainstormed ideas were seemingly forced into a category but merited a unique space. It is common for the number of channels to be increased or reduced during this process. Interestingly, in this case, the group revised the channel names through the process, but the number of channels remained at five, and the essence of those five channels remained largely unchanged throughout the process. This was likely due to some research by the adult teaching pastor leading to suggested ideas that simply turned out to work well for this ministry design. When this exercise was final, the list of categories with the relevant ideas of what participants should know and be able to do as a result of participating in the Adult Teaching Ministry became the channels of ministry around which the intended outcomes would be crafted.

Channels of Ministry – Adult Teaching Ministry

Spiritual Formation

Biblical and Church History

Theology

Christian Living

Leadership

Brainstormed Knowledge and Skills Aligned to Channels of Ministry – Adult Teaching Ministry

Spiritual Formation
Sound doctrine
Spiritual formation
Baptism and Lord's Supper
Worldview

Biblical and Church History
Biblical history
Meta-narrative of Scripture

Theology
Tenets of orthodox theology
Exegesis
Holy Spirit
Connect Old Testament and New Testament
Loci of theology

Christian Living
Personal testimony of conversion
Spiritual disciplines

The Bible and life
Living out the Christian life
Evangelism
Spiritual gifts/giftedness

Leadership
Learning to lead
Biblical view of leadership
Mentoring
Community outreach

Spiritual Engagement

Mission, Vision, and Core Values

Philosophy

Channels

Intended Outcomes

Evaluation

Applications and Activities

Philosophy

Mission, Vision, and Core Values

Spiritual Engagement

With the channels of ministry established, the project participants were then asked to develop a series of formal outcome statements that capsulized each of the brainstormed ideas of what participants should know and be able to do as a result of participating in the Adult Teaching Ministry and formalized them into measurable goals for the ministry. This part of the process was well served by having a facilitator knowledgeable in curriculum design and adept at crafting measurable outcome statements that applied Bloom's taxonomy to assure a broad spectrum of engagement opportunities (Bloom, et al., 1956). Language was carefully chosen to compensate for this being an infinite ministry rather than one segmented by year-long grades or specifically defined age groups (e.g. 2-4 years of age). The infinite form of this ministry also meant that participants in the ministry would likely interact with each of the outcomes on multiple occasions. So, care was taken to design outcomes broad enough for multiple interactions while preserving the ability to measure the outcomes readily. The complex nature of drafting and wordsmithing outcome statements required inputs from all of the participants to assure that the specific language desired was integrated into the final set of outcomes. Once again, having a facilitator familiar with the design process and the methods of polishing intentions into specific language was a boon to the group. The resulting list of outcomes grouped by channel follows.

Outcomes – Adult Teaching Ministry

Spiritual Formation
- Apply sound principles to study the Bible for personal growth.
- Identify tenets of sound doctrine and the Christian faith.
- Engage effectively in the spiritual disciplines including but not limited to prayer, fasting, Bible study, reflection, and observance of the Sabbath.
- Engage in the ordinances of water baptism and the Lord's Supper.
- Explain and apply the Christian worldview.
- Share the testimony of their personal conversion.

Biblical and Church History
- Trace the history of the People of God as presented in the Old Testament.
- Explain the concept of the meta-narrative of Scripture.
- Explain key ideas of the major eras in Church history.
- Apply lessons from the Old Testament and from the history of the Christian Church.

Theology
- Explain the central tenets of orthodox Christianity.
- Explain the key ideas of the ten principle themes of Christian theology.
- Apply proper exegesis to the study of Scripture.
- Explain the Scriptural foundation of the distinctive doctrine of the denomination.

Christian Living

- Explain how Scripture offers guidance for the common challenges of life.
- Apply Biblical principles to everyday life.
- Articulate the guidance provided by Scripture for men and women to fulfill their unique roles as Christ followers.
- Create points of tangency between the Church and the community at large in order to share the Gospel.

Leadership
- Identify Biblically sound teaching on leadership.
- Engage in personal leadership development.
- Apply Biblically sound principles of leadership in home, work, church, and other settings.
- Mentor other Christ followers seeking to become leaders in the Church and community.

Once the design was completed, the channels and outcomes were shared with other members of the ministry to assure that the theology presented remained orthodox and that there would be support from colleagues and leaders throughout the ministry. Once approved, the channels of ministry served as overarching themes to guide the schedule of adult teaching classes. Leaders could focus on one channel each quarter and develop classes that addressed the channel, or they could weave the channels together offering classes that addressed multiple channels through the year. By considering the channels, leaders helped to assure that the ministry remained balanced not favoring one channel or outcome over another and, thus, helping to retain the interest and participation of the adults under the ministry. Delving deeper, then, leaders selected specific outcomes within each channel to guide the activities and interactions that would occur in the course of carrying out the ministry.

Ministry Applications and Activities

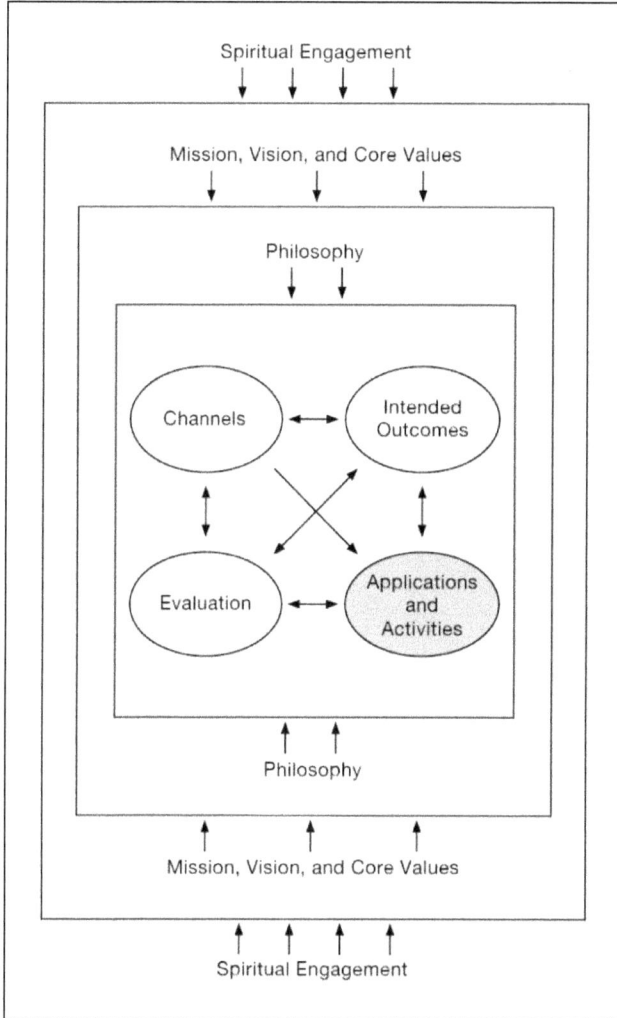

With the channels and outcomes firmly established, leaders were able to use the ministry design to determine the need for certain ongoing instructional offerings. These included a course for those new to the faith, a means of integrating new members into the church, and an ongoing discipleship plan. Channels became the intended basis of determining broad areas to address through quarterly classes. This allowed leaders to plan class schedules ahead and to secure teachers who were adequately versed in the specific channel to be addressed. Teachers could be presented the outcomes associated with the channels in time to use them as guidelines for course preparation. It was also hoped that courses developed to align with established channels and outcomes would be preserved for future use so that the constant and inefficient re-creation of courses could be discontinued.

Stage 3

Ministry/Program Evaluation

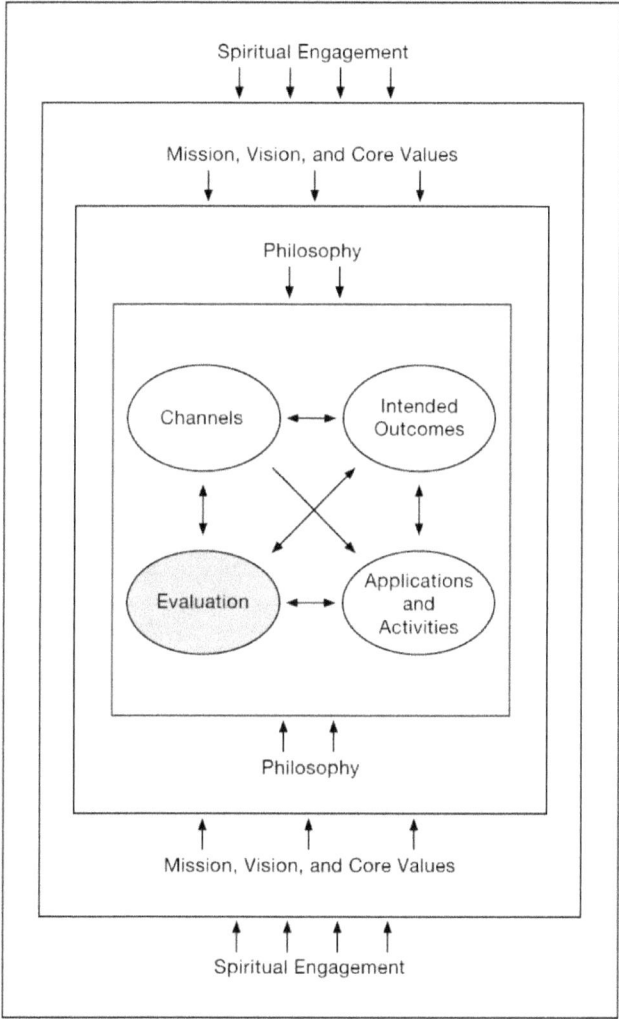

By having clear channels and outcomes, the framework for ministry evaluation was established. Outcomes were written to be measurable by a variety of formal and informal means including class attendance, participant surveys, and anecdotal (if not fully qualitative) observations. Data gathered could be used to determine which channels and outcomes were being adequately addressed and which needed additional attention.

While engaging in evaluation of the Adult Teaching Ministry, leaders opted for moving away from the traditional format of adult classes. However, the concepts represented by the channels and outcomes still served as foundational ideas in the implementation of a new approach to adult teaching.

Chapter 5:

Boomers Ministry

Background

The same church described above in the Adult Teaching
Ministry example was also beginning to use data to
determine the ministry needs of the church. That data
indicated a growing number of attendees who fit the
category of "Baby Boomers," individuals born between the
early to mid-1940s and the mid-1960s. This generation of
Americans ultimately became a large segment of the
population characterized by possessing significant
economic and political influence. As a group, they
developed distinct expectations and wielded their political
and economic influence readily. So, church leaders
perceived the necessity to draw these individuals into
meaningful relationship with the church that included
engaging their talents and resources while meeting the felt
needs of this unique segment of the population. The church
hired a full-time staff pastor to engage this group of people.
Having heard of the previous success of enacting the

Intentional Ministry Model from his colleagues, the newly hired pastor determined to engage in that process to design a meaningful plan of ministry to the Baby Boomers.

Assembling the Participants

The Boomers pastor began the conversation with the educational consultants who attended the church and had led the Adult Teaching Ministry development using the Intentional Ministry Model though they were not members of the Boomer generation. The collaborative nature of the model was explained, and the search began for willing participants to engage in the process. In early discussions with the Boomers pastor, the diversity of this generation became evident. While united somewhat by an age range that identifies the generation, at the time of this project Boomers remained unusually diverse in stage of life with some fully retired, some partially retired, and others still fully in the work force. Further, marital status varies widely across this generation including married, divorced, widowed, and single having never married. This status also created diversity in family focus with some focused on children, grandchildren, or even great-grandchildren and others viewing that experience as completely foreign. In addition were the commonly expected differences in race, gender, and socioeconomic status. With this awareness, the project participants were deliberately selected to represent these diverse segments of this generation.

Further, participants were chosen who had a vested interest in the ministry or program, a passion for ministry to this generation, and a heart to engage in the process. Church leadership had expressed a desire to launch the new ministry within the year, so, the process would need to be carried out in much less time than the design of the Adult Teaching Ministry. Participants were made aware of this goal at the outset and readily committed to the time and energy necessary for successful ministry development.

The Intentional Ministry Model

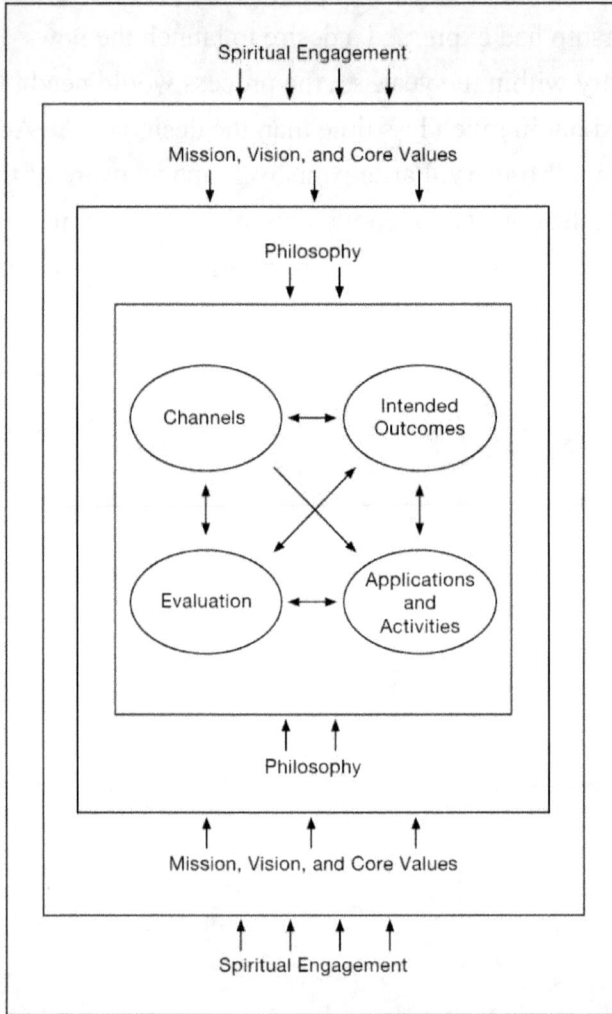

Stage 1

Spiritual Engagement

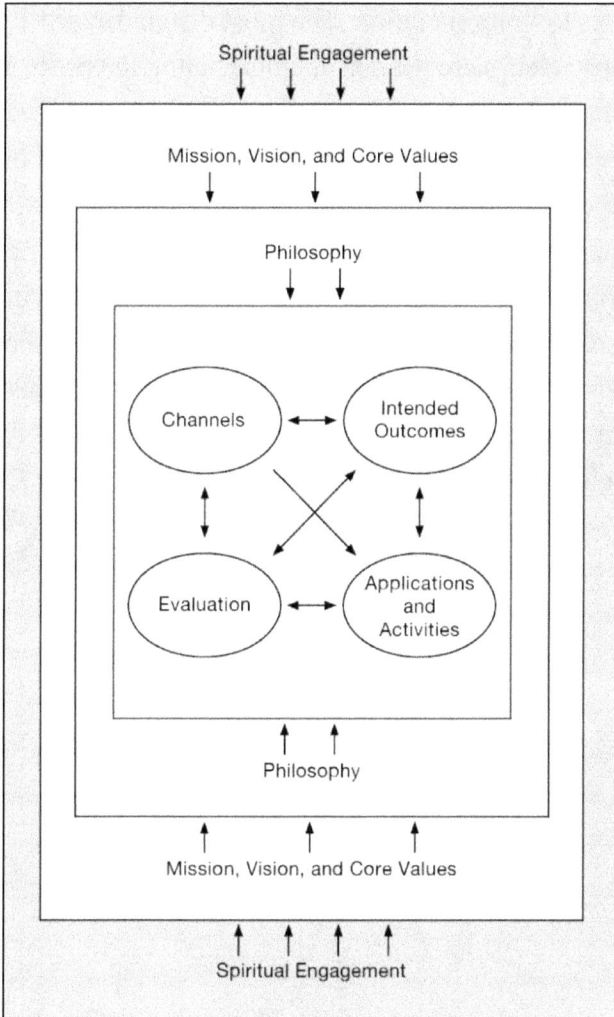

Similarly to those involved in the Adult Teaching Ministry design, spiritual engagement was relatively simple for his group of project participants. Each had a vested interest in the success of the project or carried a distinct call to minister to this generation. The most distant from the ministry itself were the consultants leading the process who, nonetheless, retained a heart for ministry and were committed to the creation of a manageable program that would endure even after the design process was complete and the consultants moved on to other projects. So, prayer, searching the Word of God, and other spiritual activities came naturally. With this project beginning with a shorter established time frame than the Adult Teaching Ministry, the participants easily remained engaged spiritually throughout the process.

Mission, Vision, and Core Values

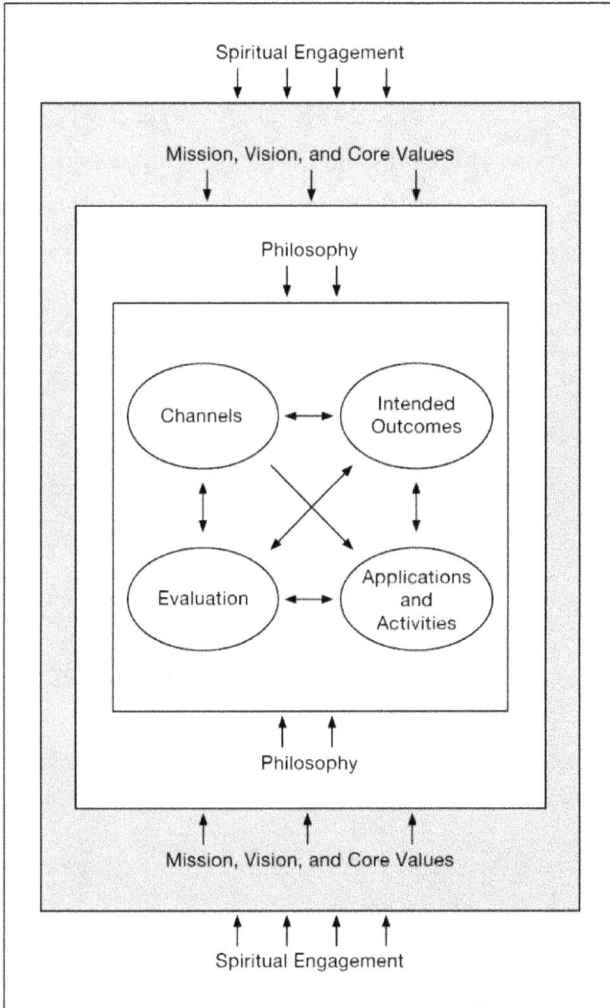

Spiritual Engagement

Mission, Vision, and Core Values

Philosophy

Channels — Intended Outcomes

Evaluation — Applications and Activities

Philosophy

Mission, Vision, and Core Values

Spiritual Engagement

As this ministry development began, the church was fully engaged and making significant progress in redefining its mission, vision, and core values. However, the design process was completed under the original mission and the transitional vision. Project participants spent a significant amount of time discussing what they perceived to be pertinent characteristics of the generation as a whole. These served as core values for the ministry; what was important to the generation was, the group determined, necessary to be important to the ministry in order for the ministry to be effective.

Mission Statement
To lead people of all ages into a life changing relationship with Jesus

Transitional Vision Statement
Connect. Grow. Serve.

Group-Created List of Core Values
Relationships
(Generation for the) Cause
Service
Meaningful Activities

Philosophy of Ministry

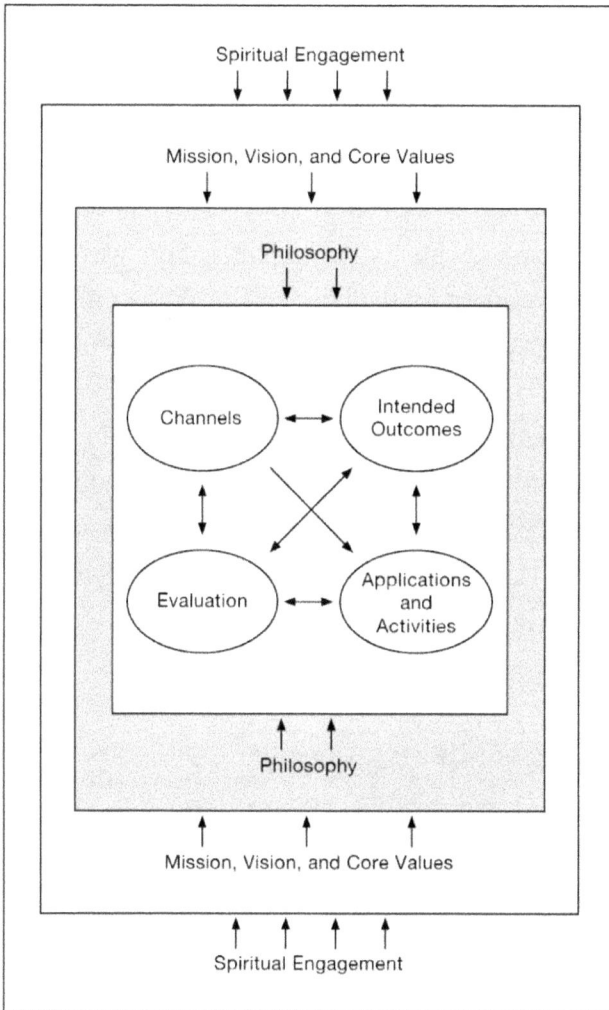

Spiritual Engagement

Mission, Vision, and Core Values

Philosophy

Channels ⟷ Intended Outcomes

Evaluation ⟷ Applications and Activities

Philosophy

Mission, Vision, and Core Values

Spiritual Engagement

During preliminary conversations about the ministry design process, it was noted to the Boomers pastor that the model needed to be grounded in a solid philosophy of ministry as well as connecting to the mission, vision, and values of the organization. With that knowledge, the pastor came prepared with a clear philosophy of ministry that was shared with the project participants allowing them to align the ministry design philosophically from the outset. This made the design process much more efficient than the Adult Teaching Ministry design since there was no delay in the process caused by the need to clarify the ministry philosophy before proceeding. Notice that the philosophy statement drifts into an action plan slightly. This was a bit concerning since the design process should allow the action plan to emerge from objective discussions around mission, vision, and philosophy. However, it ultimately was not harmful to the design process for these considerations to be brought forth early in the process.

Philosophy of Ministry – Boomers

The purpose of ministry to the Baby Boom Generation (Boomers) is to advance the larger mission and vision of the local church to that generation of individuals born roughly between the years 1946-1964 (including the "technical" Boomers who are part of the designation strictly based on age, as well as "cultural" Boomers who display similar attitudes and life-situations as the "technical" Boomers) being sensitive and responsive to the unique challenges faced and attitudes reflected by this generation of individuals.

The philosophy of this ministry is founded on the belief that growth and service are best encouraged and accomplished through strong and godly relationships. Therefore, this ministry will emphasize creating an environment of inclusion and friendship that demonstrates the value of these relationships and allows for participants to be fully engaged in the life and ministry of the larger church body.

Therefore, the Boomer ministry will provide participants the opportunity to grow in all three aspects of the church's vision including connecting in meaningful, Christ-centered relationships; growing deeper in the knowledge of God through His Word; and serving both the church and the local community. We acknowledge and agree that all three aspects of the vision are important and necessary for a healthy church body, and we remain committed to helping fulfill that vision through this ministry.

Stage 2

Channels of Ministry and Intended Outcomes

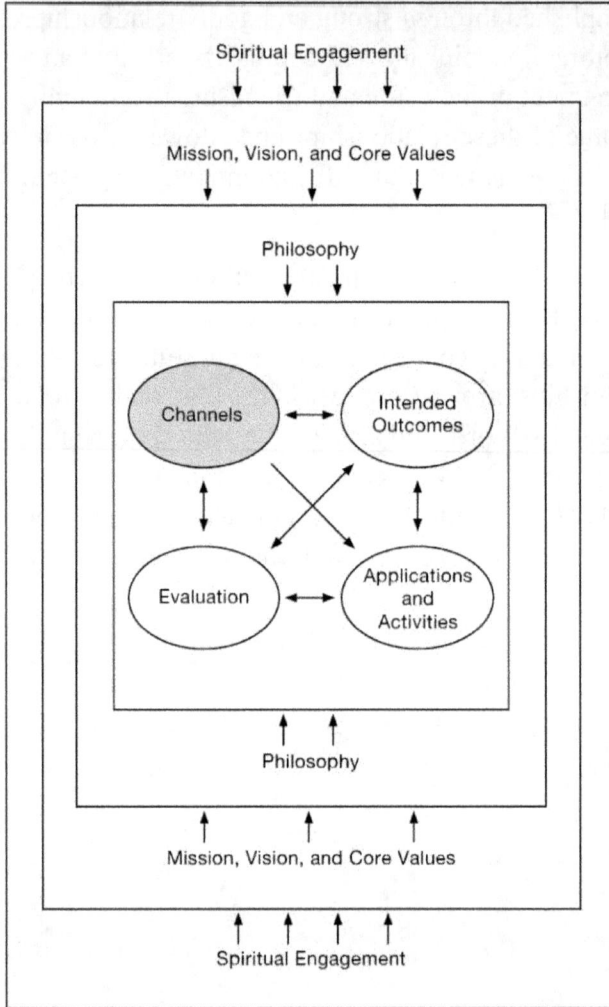

With the philosophy of ministry clearly communicated, the project participants confidently turned to the task of determining what participants should know and be able to do as a result of participating in the Boomers ministry. At this point, the notion of an infinite ministry serving congregants for potentially many years once again surfaced clearly. Project participants had to grapple with the concept that there was no end to this ministry; those served by the ministry would always be Boomers though they would, as a group, continue to mature both physically and, hopefully, spiritually. Like the Adult Teaching Ministry, the Boomers ministry had, through its mission, vision, core values, and philosophy established a clear commitment to address the needs of a highly diverse group of participants. The infinite nature of the ministry exerted a significant influence on the intended outcomes that were developed for this ministry just as it had on the Adult Teaching Ministry design.

As with the Adult Teaching Ministry, the project participants began by brainstorming what they wanted Boomers to know and be able to do as a result of interacting with (notice that the notion was not that of *completing*) the ministry. That list is below. No idea was discarded, and no judgments passed on ideas at this point, though the facilitator did have to help project participants remain focused on the brainstorming task at hand deflecting some interesting conversations for a later time in the process. At this point in the process, the purpose was simply to capture all of the ideas for future evaluation and classification. If an idea sounded familiar to one already mentioned, the participants paused to consider if the ideas were the same or if there were subtle differences between them. In either case, the idea was captured by a new item in the list or as a marking indicating the duplication. As noted in the earlier example, duplication can be a signal of two things: it can either indicate that the idea is significant enough to be mentioned multiple times and needs to be given the due attention, or it can signify that the brainstorming is coming to a close. As the facilitator began to notice a longer lag between the offering of ideas from the participants and significant duplication of ideas, the participants were queried regarding whether they believed they had exhausted all of the ideas. Once each of the participants indicated an end to personal contributions, the brainstorming session drew to a conclusion. Unlike the Adult Teaching Ministry design, the brainstorming session for this project was completed in a single, highly focused session. Nonetheless, the opportunity for participants to add to the list at a later time was clearly expressed; the Intentional Ministry Model is an iterative model, so the revisiting of a stage or step in the process can occur at any time.

Partial List of Brainstormed Knowledge and Skills – Boomers Ministry
Relationships
Cause

Social Events
Be Real and Safe
Varied Lifestyles and Needs
Meaningful Activities
Mindful of Time
Give Back
Sever Rather than Be Served
Lead the Next Generations
Spirit Led
Evangelism
Power of the Generation

As in the Adult Teaching Ministry, once the brainstorming concluded, participants were asked to begin grouping ideas into sets of similar themes. The use of "sticky notes" helped facilitate this process as brainstormed ideas placed one per note were readily able to be moved by participants. Electronic tools are also available to facilitate this process. Categories were named once enough items were placed in each group to demonstrate its theme; this group chose to adopt as categories the concepts of the transitional vision statement: "Connect," "Grow," and "Serve." Once each and every brainstormed idea was placed in a category, the participants were asked to consider if any of the categories could be combined. Once that part of the process was completed, participants were asked to consider if, in light of the existing categories, there were any that might be missing or if any of the brainstormed ideas were seemingly forced into a category but merited a unique space. The group identified "Leadership" as needing its own category. When this exercise was final, the list of categories with the relevant ideas of what participants should know and be able to do as a result of participating in the Boomers ministry became the channels of ministry around which the intended outcomes would be crafted. The categorization process took one full meeting session.

Channels of Ministry – Boomers Ministry

Connect

Grow

Serve

Lead

Brainstormed Knowledge and Skills Aligned to Channels of Ministry – Boomers Ministry

Connect
Relationships
Social Events
Be Real and Safe
Meaningful Activities
Mindful of Time

Grow
Varied Lifestyles and Needs
Servant Leadership
Spirit Led

Knowledge and Skills Aligned (cont.)

Serve
Cause
Give Back
Sever Rather than Be Served
Evangelism
Develop an Attitude of Service

Lead
Lead the Next Generations
Power of the Generation

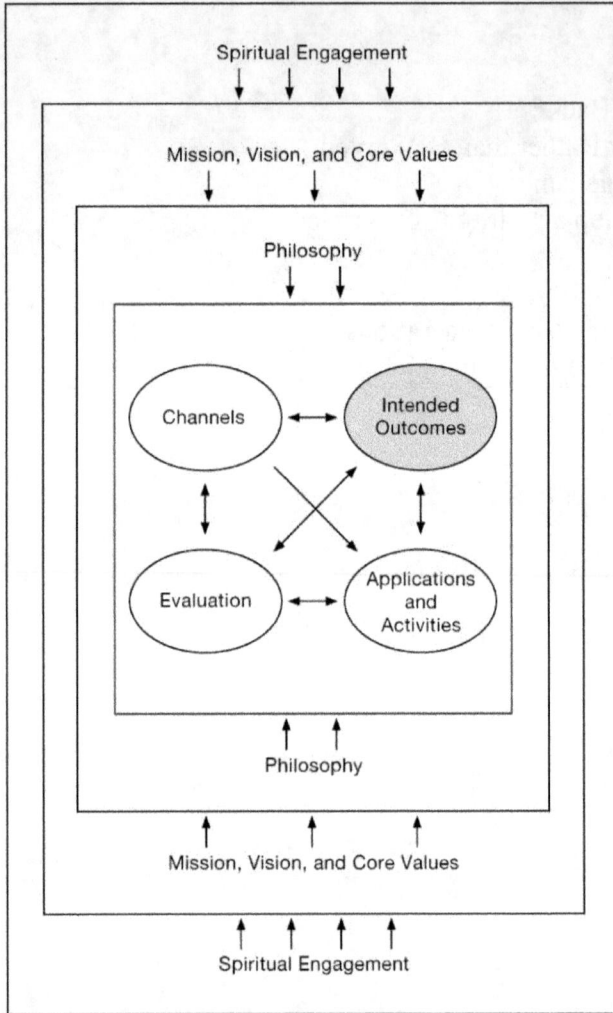

With the channels of ministry established, the project participants were then asked to develop a series of formal outcome statements that capsulized each of the brainstormed ideas of what participants should know and be able to do as a result of participating in the Boomers ministry and formalized them into measurable goals for the ministry. This part of the process was well served by having a facilitator knowledgeable in curriculum design and adept at crafting measurable outcome statements that applied Bloom's taxonomy to assure a broad spectrum of engagement opportunities (Bloom, et al., 1956). Language was carefully chosen to compensate for this being an infinite ministry. Similar to the Adult Teaching Ministry, this was not one segmented by year-long grades. However, it did, by its nature, target a particular age group. Nonetheless, there was not a point of "graduation" where one would leave this ministry; it was targeted to a generation, membership in which is by birth and not by artificial grouping such as elementary school grades. The infinite form of this ministry also meant that participants in the ministry would, as in the Adult Teaching Ministry, likely interact with each of the outcomes on multiple occasions. So, care was taken to design outcomes broad enough for multiple interactions while preserving the ability to measure the outcomes readily. The complex nature of drafting and wordsmithing outcome statements required inputs from all of the participants to assure that the specific language desired was integrated into the final set of outcomes. Once again, having a facilitator familiar with the design process and the methods of polishing intentions into specific language was a boon to the group. The resulting list of outcomes grouped by channel follows.

Outcomes – Boomers Ministry

Connect
- Build personal connections that draw the un-churched both into relationship with Christ and into the life of the Church.
- Provide a sense of belonging with people of like faith and age.
- Provide opportunities for deeper relationships.
- Create shared experiences that lead to shared culture and values.
- Develop a sense of accountability to one another and the God.

Grow

- Create a learning environment where people can practice relationship skills that translate to relationships outside of the Church.
- Train believers to engage in lifestyle evangelism.
- Model Spirit-led behavior in order to develop individuals who will both listen to and act on the leading of the Holy Spirit.
- Develop servant leaders who can carry out the work of the ministry as it expands.

Serve

- Develop an attitude of service in group members.
- Utilize shared experiences as a means to serve others both within and outside of the group.
- Encourage members to act on Spirit-led

promptings to carry out acts of service.
- Reach out to the "walking wounded" in the Church.

Lead

- Engage servant leaders to lead segments of the ministry as the work expands.
- Harness the spiritual and political power of the group to lead and influence.

As with the Adult Teaching Ministry, once the design was completed, the channels and outcomes were shared with other members of the ministry to assure that the theology presented remained orthodox and that there would be support from colleagues and leaders throughout the ministry. Once approved, the channels of ministry served as overarching themes to guide the activities that would be conducted by the ministry. Leaders could focus on specific channels as desired, or they could weave the channels together offering events and opportunities that addressed multiple channels through the year. By considering the channels, leaders helped to assure that the ministry remained balanced not favoring one channel or outcome over another and, thus, helping to retain the interest and participation of those under the ministry. In the language of the group, this allowed them to do more than just "chips and salsa" events. Delving deeper, then, leaders selected specific outcomes within each channel to guide the activities and interactions that would occur in the course of carrying out the ministry. Each activity, then, while remaining engaging for the participants, retained a clear intention and focus that helped leaders achieve ministry goals.

Ministry Applications and Activities

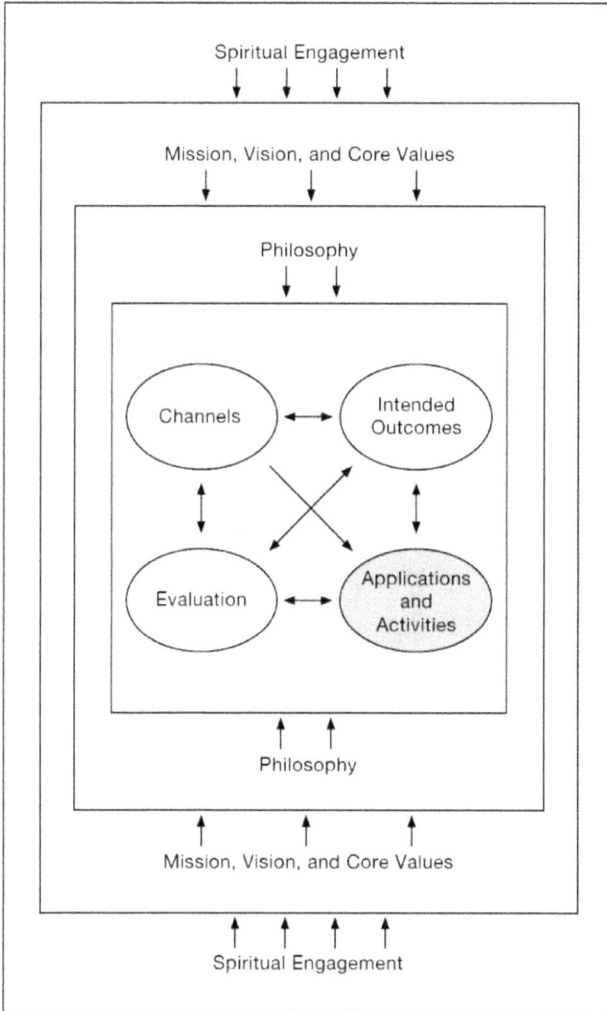

With the channels and outcomes firmly established, leaders were able to use the ministry design to determine the need for certain activities. These included a not only social events but also opportunities to learn and grow in the faith as well as to serve others. Channels became the intended basis of determining broad areas to address through the activities and prevented the ministry from losing its broader focus and becoming merely a series of social events. Conversely, the channels prevented losing sight of the need and desire for meaningful social interaction. This allowed leaders to plan ahead and to secure the necessary volunteers who were, then, adequately versed in the specific channel to be addressed and charged with retaining the foci of the activities being conducted.

Stage 3

Ministry/Program Evaluation

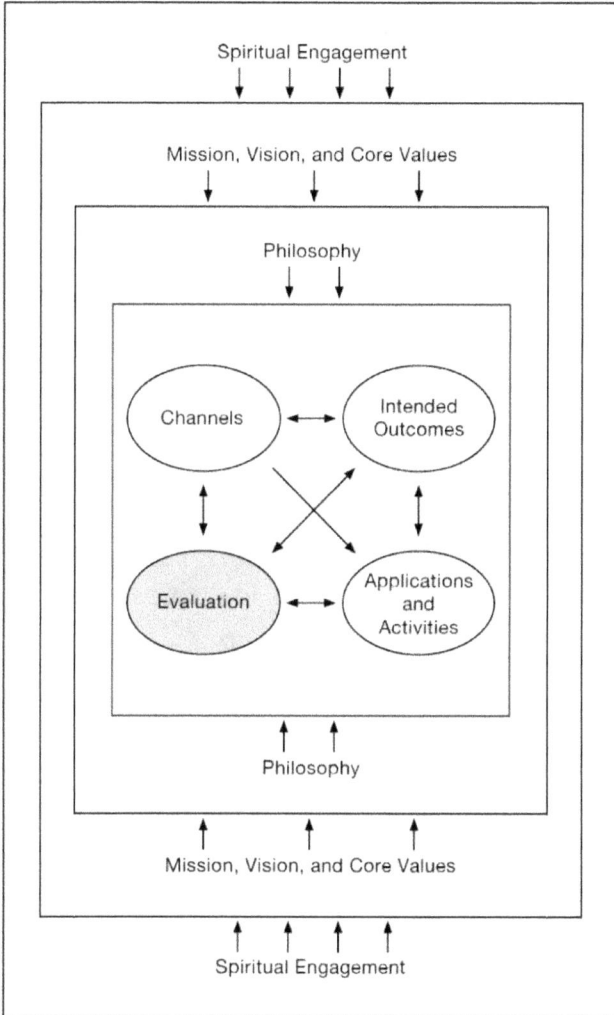

By having clear channels and outcomes, the framework for ministry evaluation was established. Outcomes were written to be measurable by a variety of formal and informal means including event attendance, participant surveys, and anecdotal (if not fully qualitative) observations. Data gathered could be used to determine which channels and outcomes were being adequately addressed and which needed additional attention. Thus, the endless string of "chips and salsa" events was avoided. While those events still had their place in the ministry (indeed, the idea of social interaction was a deliberate part of the ministry design), they did not dominate the operation of the ministry thus permitting a more balanced approach to ministering to this unique group of individuals.

As of the last contact with this group, the Boomers ministry was a vibrant part of the church with participants serving in a variety of capacities in addition to their participation in the activities of the Boomers ministry.

References

Bloom, B. S., Engelhart, M. D., Furst, E. J., Hill, W. H., & Krathwohl, D. R. (1956). *Taxonomy of educational objectives: The classification of educational goals. Handbook I: Cognitive domain.* New York: David McKay Company.

Gaebelein, F. E. (1985). The pattern of God's truth: The integration of faith and learning. Winona Lake, IN: BMH Books.

Wiggins, G., & McTighe, J. (1998). *Understanding by design.* Alexandria, VA: Association for Supervision and Curriculum Development.

www.ingramcontent.com/pod-product-compliance
Lightning Source LLC
LaVergne TN
LVHW021505080426
835509LV00018B/2414